PUERTO RICO'S BIRDS
IN PHOTOGRAPHS

A Complete Guide
Including the Virgin Islands

Mark W. Oberle

Second edition, expanded

EDITORIAL HUMANITAS
Seattle, Washington

Acknowledgements

The initial group that conceived of this project included Giff Beaton, José Ramos Gómez, José F. Cordero, and Mark W. Oberle. Advice and assistance were especially helpful from the past presidents of the Sociedad Ornitológica Puertorriqueña (SOPI), Carlos Ruiz Lebrón and Leopoldo Miranda Castro.

Without the contributions from over 80 photographers, this publication would not be possible. The 1,900 photos of theirs that we have included on the CD-ROM represent the cumulative result of thousands of hours in the field and are gratefully acknowledged in the photo credits on page 128.

Similarly, audio and video were contributed by many individuals including Barb Beck, Lindsey Brown, Larry Bryan, David Deifik, Roy DeWitt, John Faaborg, Sky and Anne Hilts, Hank Golet, Elaine and Norman Hopgood, Nicholas P. Kalodimos, Greg Lasley, William A. Mackin, Ken Meyer, Martin J. Muller, Mark Oberle, John Quantro, Rafael Rodríguez Mojica, Jorge Saliva, Martyn Stewart, and Doug Von Gausig.

Wayne Arendt, Giff Beaton, Eli Elder, Haynes Miller, Raul Pérez-Rivera, José J. Placer, Carlos Ruiz Lebrón, Jorge Saliva, and Genie Silver helped with manuscript review.

José J. Placer translated the text for the CD-ROM, and Georgann Schmalz contributed two chapters on birdwatching skills.

Greg Budney, Brad Coryell, Bob Grotke, Miriam Herrero, Pat Hood, Jeremiah Jester, Jane Jeszeck, Walter Knapp, Alice Manos, Dan McComb, Martin McClellan, William P. Oberle, José J. Placer, Yovanni Ruiz, Robert Santos, and Wally Wilhoite provided essential advice and help in preparing the CD-ROM.

We appreciate the assistance in field work and information access from Hernán Abreu, Jon Andrew, Tony Ayala, Edward L. Baker, Jr., Paul Blake, Patty Bruce, José A. Camacho, Franco Carrión, Mark and Susan Churchill, Sergio Colón López, Elizabeth Cromwell, José Cruz, Jack C. Eitniear, Axel Elfner, Craig Faanes, Pedro Fernández, Martin Frost, John Fulton, Ricardo García, Laredo González, Chris Haney, Peter Hodum,

Puerto Rican Tody

Chuck Hunter, Gary Kratt, Carol Lambert, David Lee, Allen Lewis, María López, Alexis Martínez, Hope McCourt, Bret Medders, Haynes Miller, Britta Muiznieks, Eric Nielsen, Fernando Núñez, David A. Oberle, Niña T. Oberle, William S. Oberle, Julia Parrish, Gary Phillips, Ángel Plaza, Ada Nilsa Pomales, Bill Pranty, José Rigau Pérez, Pedro Luis Ruiz, José Salguero, Aurora Sastre, Charles Siegel (Dallas Zoo), James W. Stratton, Greg Toffic, Pablo Torres, Rusty and Cheryl Trump, Ricardo Valentín, Agustín Valido, Luis Vázquez, Eduardo Ventosa, Helena Wood, and Joseph Wunderle, Jr.

We benefited from the support of the Nuttall Ornithological Club, the Sociedad Ornitológica Puertorriqueña and the Georgia Ornithological Society. Special thanks go to Mardie L. Oberle and William P. Oberle, for their encouragement and support.

Front cover photo credits, clockwise from upper left: Antillean Euphonia * (John Faaborg), Puerto Rican Parrot * (U.S. Fish & Wildlife Service), Troupial * (Bruce Hallett), Prothonotary Warbler (Giff Beaton), Puerto Rican Tody * (John Faaborg), Puerto Rican Screech-Owl * (Mark Oberle), Puerto Rican Spindalis (Mark Oberle).
Cover Art: Miriam Herrero, Robert Santos, Mark Oberle.

PUERTO RICO'S BIRDS IN PHOTOGRAPHS

A Complete Guide and CD-ROM Including the Virgin Islands

TABLE OF CONTENTS

Introduction

This publication is designed for students, tourists, and anyone who wants to understand Puerto Rico's natural heritage by learning about its birds. Along the way, there are important lessons for conservation of our natural resources. We have written the text in a non-technical style to describe individual species in ways that are understandable to the general reader. The book contains photos of 185 species---all the birds that a casual observer or serious birdwatcher might see, plus many rarer species of special interest. The text emphasizes birds that breed in Puerto Rico. In addition, the common, non-breeding visitors are illustrated with photographs, but have a more limited text account since information on their life histories is readily available in publications listed in the bibliography.

More than most book projects, our effort represents a truly cooperative enterprise. In 1995, when our original publisher, Dr. Pepe Ramos, saw Giff Beaton's photographs of Puerto Rican birds, he was amazed at the tremendous variety of colorful species that surrounded him without his knowledge. He was also surprised to learn that nobody had produced a complete publication of photographs of Puerto Rico's birds. The two previous photo books related to Puerto Rico dealt with limited groups of species: Jorge Saliva's book on birds of Vieques and Pedro Ortiz Rosas' book on gamebirds. Having recognized this gap, we decided to embark on a photographic effort, to alert both residents and visitors to Puerto Rico's wildlife heritage. However, it was only during my sabbatical

Puerto Rican Screech-Owl

year that I was able to put in the time to pull this collaboration together. And "collaboration" is the key word. Although one person wrote the text, dozens of people have contributed photographs. The photo editors---Giff Beaton, Carlos Ruiz and I---have tried to select the best photos available.

The bilingual CD-ROM covers all of Puerto Rico's 350 species, with 1,600 additional photos, more detailed species accounts, plus audio of 330 species. Updates and corrections will be posted on the web at www.puertoricobirds.com. We welcome additional photos, audio and video from readers. So please contact us if you would like to contribute to future editions of this book and CD-ROM.

Mark W. Oberle
Box 357230
University of Washington
Seattle WA 98195-7230
oberle@mindspring.com

Magnificent Frigatebird

Puerto Rico's Birds

Birds have always fascinated human beings because of their song, colorful plumage, and ability to fly. They communicate by sound and sight, much as humans do. In contrast, many mammal species are nocturnal, and use smell and high frequency sound to communicate---senses that have deteriorated in humans as we have evolved. Birds also lead us to an appreciation of the interconnectedness, fragility, and uniqueness of life. These qualities can be easier to understand in our island environment than in a continental one. Learning about birds in our immediate environment also has much to teach us about how radically our environment has changed in recent centuries. To preserve our rich natural heritage for future generations to enjoy, it is important to learn from the errors of history, as well as the successes of conservation efforts. Understanding birds and their populations can give us insights into how best to live in harmony with nature.

While most human beings spend time learning about our own species, *Homo sapiens*, we still know little about the life history of the plants and animals that surround us, and on which we depend for survival. In times past, we humans have focused on birds as agricultural pests or objects for hunting, but more people now study birds with binoculars than with shotguns. There are about 9,800 species of birds worldwide, each with its own communication strategy, mating system, and unique adaptations to survival on this planet. Yet we know very little about the behavior and survival strategies of most species. To put this in perspective, there are about 300 billion individual birds in the world, and only 6 billion humans. It is time we got to know our neighbors.

The avifauna of Puerto Rico and the Virgin Islands includes 350 species of birds. However, a third are "accidentals" (stragglers that have only been reported a few times). Also, 35 of the total bird species have been introduced by man, but many of these may not have established sustainable breeding populations. About 120 bird species regularly nest in Puerto Rico, including native species, plus other birds that have been introduced by humans over the last few centuries. Sixteen of Puerto Rico's nesting species are considered "endemic" to Puerto Rico---that is, they are basically found nowhere else (although a few of these also occur in the Virgin Islands).

Also, scientists soon may "create" two other species endemic to Puerto Rico, once taxonomists decide whether to elevate the island's subspecies to full species status. These are currently called the Lesser Antillean Pewee and the Greater Antillean Oriole.

Puerto Rican Parrot

In addition to the local nesting avifauna, many other species of birds breed in North America and elsewhere, but spend the winter in the tropics, including Puerto Rico and other islands in the Caribbean.

Biogeography and Evolution of Birds in the West Indies

Puerto Rico is an incubator of evolution, with 16 surviving endemic birds on an island only 100 by 35 miles. (Puerto Rico's maximum dimensions are 111 by 39 miles.) In the U.S.A., by comparison, the contiguous 48 states have 900 times as much land area, but only 10 surviving endemic bird species. The reason that Puerto Rico is blessed with so many unique species is that islands provide unique habitat conditions and the geographic isolation that are necessary for populations of animals and plants to slowly evolve into new species. For details on Caribbean bird evolution, see the book by Lack in the bibliography.

5

Magnificent Frigatebird

Extinction: The Big Picture

A common error in discussions on extinction is the argument that: "Since extinction of species and survival of the fittest are normal features of natural evolution, then we humans should not be concerned about extinction of other species." This belief has a deceptive shred of truth to it, but is based on a distorted perspective of history. Over the last 500 million years there have been five mass extinction events when large numbers of species became extinct within a very short period. The most famous of these was the last "completed" extinction event that featured the disappearance of the dinosaurs 65 million years ago. But during most of Earth's history, natural extinction rates have been much lower than during the five mass extinction events.

We are currently in the middle of the sixth major extinction event in geological history. However, this one is not caused by comet impacts, volcanic eruptions, or natural climate fluctuations, but rather by our expanding human population and its resulting impact on natural resources. Right now, the extinction rate is 100-1000 times higher than the baseline rate in 99% of Earth's history. Worldwide, we

Limpkin

are losing about 50,000 species of plants and animals a year. The natural rate of extinction of birds worldwide during most of their history on Earth is on the order of one species in a thousand years. During the last few thousand years, approximately 2000 species of birds have become extinct—one sixth of the total number of all bird species. This dramatic increase in extinctions may be partly due to climate change, but mostly due to the expansion of human populations, especially into virgin, island habitats. Some 12 percent of the Earth's 9,800 bird species are now threatened with extinction.

The current mass extinction period has had two phases. First, has been the expansion of humans into isolated islands, including Australia, New Zealand, other Pacific Islands, and the Caribbean. Humans have extinguished other species either directly through hunting, or indirectly through habitat changes or introductions of exotic animals like cats, rats, mosquitoes or disease organisms. Islands often contain many species that have lost their defenses against predators and diseases, and many island birds have lost the ability to fly. The Dodo (*Raphus cucullatus*) of Mauritius Island is the most well-known example of a flightless species doomed to extinction soon after contact with humans. In most island groups, humans (or their accompanying rats, domestic animals or diseases) have wiped out large numbers of native species soon after humans arrived. In Hawaii, 70 of the 140 endemic land bird species have been extinguished since humans arrived there 1,600 years ago. Of the surviving 70 species, 30 are now endangered.

The second phase of the current mass extinction event is the destruction of species on large continental landmasses due to widespread expansion of humans, with our increasing pressures on habitats and direct impacts on wildlife populations. The com-

6

monest bird at the time of Columbus was the Passenger Pigeon (*Ectopistes migratorius*) of North America, with a population estimated in the billions. Market hunting and destruction of the bird's habitat eradicated it from the planet by 1914.

Puerto Rico has not escaped the sixth mass extinction, although the specific causes of an individual species' extinction may never be known. At least 5 endemic birds have become extinct in recent millenia in Puerto Rico---as many as in all of North America. Some of these recent extinctions may have been caused by climate change, others by the Taino Indians, while still other extinctions were recently precipitated by modern inhabitants. Puerto Rico had a large flightless rail that was hunted by the Taino Indians, an endemic snipe, an endemic quail-dove, an endemic barn owl, and an endemic finch. In addition, several subspecies in Puerto Rico have become extinct recently. Some species that still survive elsewhere are now extinct in Puerto Rico. For example, the White-necked Crow ("Cuervo pescueciblanco," *Corvus leucognaphalus*) was hunted to extinction in Puerto Rico by the mid-20th Century, but survives on Hispaniola. The Limpkin ("Carrao," *Aramus guarauna,* photo p. 6) was still hunted in the 19th Century in Puerto Rico, but has only rarely been reported on this island recently. Since bird bones are quite fragile and easily destroyed, we may never know about other species that have become extinct in recent centuries, but have left no trace.

These extinct species---some of which were once common birds---should remind all of us that we cannot take for granted that our children will have the benefit of interacting with the same birds that co-occupy this planet with us now. If it were not for significant efforts by conservationists starting in the 1960s, the endemic Puerto Rican Parrot and the endemic Yellow-shouldered Blackbird would almost certainly be extinct on Puerto Rico. These sustained efforts require significant resources in the short term, but hopefully these species will recover and allow future generations of Puerto Ricans and visitors to enjoy their company and learn more about them.

Unfortunately we know little about how the Taino Indians interacted with the natural world after they arrived in Puerto Rico. But we do know that the Iroquois and other North American tribes traditionally included in major decisions the needs of their descendants, seven generations into the future. This "seventh-generational thinking"---taking into account the long-term, cumulative impact of land use and other resource decisions---needs to become a standard part of our decision-making process. We need to apply a seventh-generational mode of thinking to combat Earth's sixth mass extinction event

Migratory Birds

People often talk about the birds in their neighborhood as "our" birds. But in fact, we often share "our" birds with people from other countries part of the year. Some of the commonest winter birds in Puerto Rico, such as Northern Parula, Black-and-White Warbler, Prairie Warbler, American Redstart, and Belted Kingfisher, are migratory species that nest in North America. These species are important members of the avian community in Puerto Rico, and some even spend more time on their winter grounds than on the breeding grounds. Thus, conservation and land management decisions in Puerto Rico may affect the abundance and survival of these birds not just on the island, but on their breeding range as well. Most migrants from

Indigo Bunting

North America that come to the Caribbean stop at larger islands closer to the mainland. The result is that migrant species decrease in abundance on islands farther east in the Caribbean.

There are also a few species that breed in Puerto Rico, yet despite the subtropical climate, migrate elsewhere for part of the year. For example, the Black-whiskered Vireo, Antillean Nighthawk, and Caribbean Martin are common breeding species, but most individuals leave Puerto Rico to winter in Central

Brown Pelicans

or South America. This behavior may be a holdover from the Ice Age when the climate in Puerto Rico was much cooler than it is today. There are also some terns and other seabirds that nest in Puerto Rico but move hundreds or thousands of miles out to sea when they are not breeding.

Many migrant landbird species have declined recently. For example, Prairie Warbler populations have declined by over 50% in the last thirty years on the breeding range in North America. The reasons for these declines vary from species to species, and may depend on a complex interaction of factors on breeding grounds, winter grounds, and at migration stopover sites where birds "refuel" to continue their migration.

Conservation Issues Affecting Puerto Rican Birds

Many of the ecosystems that Puerto Rico's birds depend upon are threatened, and this threat will continue to increase without public support for conservation efforts. Conservation in Puerto Rico is important not just to preserve the island's own natural heritage, but also to support ecosystems in other regions where migrant species spend part of the year. The section that follows gives examples of some threats that affect Puerto Rico's birds. For more details on issues and possible solutions, see the books by Raffaele, and by Greenberg and Reaser, listed on page 127.

• Land use: Direct human alteration of habitat is one of the most important factors affecting wildlife populations. Where people live and work, and how they use resources have direct impacts on wildlife habitat. Puerto Rico has an accelerating pattern of rural development, as Puerto Ricans commute to

cities from ever more distant suburbs, and more and more retirees from Puerto Rico and the U.S. mainland chose to live in rural Puerto Rico. More than a third of Puerto Rico's farmland has been converted to other uses in the last few decades. Between 1962 and 1997 farmland declined from 1.9 million acres to 1.3 million acres, although a small portion of farmland conversion was to forestland. A few native birds, and many exotic birds, benefit from urban development, but many native forest birds decline with urbanization. Another example of the impact of land use decisions on birds is solid waste disposal. Puerto Rico now generates 8,100 tons of garbage per day. This creates pressure for landfills that remove land from wildlife habitat for decades, especially in low-lying areas.

• Deforestation: Most of Puerto Rico was forested in Columbus' time, and well into the early 19th Century. But by the early 20th Century, only 1% of Puerto Rico's original forest remained. Later, as Puerto Rico became more urbanized, much farmland and pasture reverted to secondary forest. As a result, Puerto Rico was almost 40% forested by the late 20th Century. Unfortunately, subsequent land-use policies and practices have led to increased deforestation in the last decade, with more than 0.6% of forestlands destroyed on the island per year. Only 28,000 acres of forest are officially preserved in the Caribbean National Forest (El Yunque). The 25 Commonwealth forests and reserves protect only 90,000 acres of forest and marshlands. On a positive note, many West Indian birds evolved to accommodate hurricanes, and thus have sprung back relatively quickly as forests recovered.

• Wetland destruction: Wetland loss has

8

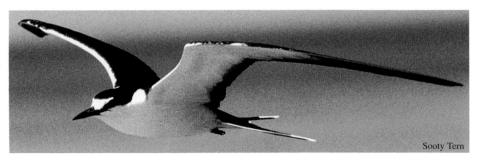

Sooty Tern

been severe in Puerto Rico, with perhaps half of the original mangrove stands destroyed, and many natural fresh and saltwater marshes drained or converted to agriculture. Although some marshlands have been converted to artificial lakes or ponds, many of these man-made impoundments, such as golf course ponds, are relatively simple ecosystems that support only a few bird species.

• Agricultural practices: Changes in agricultural practices impact birds both positively and negatively. The clearing of forest for farmland a century ago favored birds of open fields at the expense of forest species. Excessive use of fertilizer results in runoff of excess nitrogen into lakes, streams, marshes, and estuaries, and disrupts aquatic ecosystems. One controversial development is the subsidized conversion of coffee grown under shade trees to "sun coffee." This practice removes the shade trees that many breeding birds and migrants utilize. See this web site for details: http://nationalzoo.si.edu/ConservationAndScience/MigratoryBirds/.

• Pesticides: DDT was an essential insecticide in the campaign that eradicated malaria from Puerto Rico in the 1950s, but it and other long-acting pesticides severely reduced reproductive success in pelicans, ospreys, and several other bird species. Although DDT is no longer legally used in Puerto Rico, other agricultural chemicals and industrial toxins harm birds and other wildlife in ways that are only now becoming clear. For example, some chemicals even in small amounts can mimic estrogen hormones, and seriously reduce reproductive success.

• Hunting and egg collecting: Taking of birds or their eggs may have been the direct cause of the extinction of several birds on the island. Many seabird nesting areas were severely impacted by commercial egg collecting. Populations of many ducks, sandpipers, and parrots are much lower now than a century ago in part because of indiscriminate hunt-

ing. Although modern hunting regulations are designed to maintain population levels, illegal hunting still occurs. The federal Migratory Bird Treaty Act applies to Puerto Rico and the U.S. Virgin Islands, and prohibits the killing, possession, transportation, and importation of migratory birds, their eggs, feathers, and nests.

• Pet trade: Many native species, especially parrots, have been under severe pressure from collectors for sale to pet stores and exporters. The possession of native species is illegal, and the capture of exotic birds in Puerto Rico is regulated by the Departamento de Recursos Naturales y Ambientales.

• Introduced predators: The mongoose ("mangosta," *Herpestes auropunctatus*) was introduced to control rodents in sugarcane plantations, and is now a major threat to ground-nesting birds. Introduced roof rats (*Rattus rattus*) are found throughout the island and are a plague even to tree-nesting species. A very sensitive subject is the common practice of allowing cats (*Felis catus*) to wander outdoors where they kill thousands of birds a year in Puerto Rico. A campaign called "Cats Indoors!" is aimed at persuading cat owners and local governments to keep cats away from wild birds. For details, see: www.abcbirds.org/cats/.

• Introduced diseases can affect birds directly or indirectly. For example, a wood-boring crustacean, *Sphaeroma terebrans*, hitchhiked on wooden ships a century ago and now

Puerto Rican Spindalis

Yellow Warbler

kills mangrove root tips throughout the western Atlantic. This limits the spread of mangroves toward the ocean, and reduces this threatened habitat for birds and other species.

• Collision hazards: Power lines, large antennae, aircraft, cars, and glass windows kill birds whose flight paths intersect these dangers.

• Exotic species: Non-native plants and animals directly or indirectly affect native birds by altering habitat or directly competing, often in ways that may take decades to gradually become apparent.

• Destruction of reefs: Coral reef destruction has had an impact on fish populations and the seabirds that feed in coastal waters. About 2/3 of the world's coral reefs have been degraded, and those in Puerto Rico are in serious trouble. Overfishing, sedimentation, pollution, sea temperature rise, hurricanes, and direct damage to reefs by ships' anchors and construction projects have contributed to these declines.

• Oil spills and seepage: Worldwide, over 3 million tons of oil are spilled into the sea annually. Birds are affected both by the energy loss and stress when oil contaminates feathers, and by direct toxicity when they ingest oil while they preen. Because oil separation equipment is expensive to operate, ship owners and crews are often tempted to discharge waste oil illegally at sea. In 1998, the U.S. Coast Guard fined one cruise ship company a record $9 million for systematically dumping waste oil at sea off Puerto Rico.

• Climate change: The "greenhouse" warming of the Earth's atmosphere due to fossil fuel burning and the human production of other gases that trap heat is predicted to increase the frequency of strong hurricanes and to raise sea level. Sea level rose 18 centimeters in the 20th Century and may be rising faster now.

• Population growth: Although newspaper articles and other public discussions usually focus on individual conservation issues, human population growth is an underlying factor in all of the individual threats to wildlife populations. In general, the larger the human population is in any given area, the larger the cumulative impact of any one threat, and the greater the demand on a specific resource. After losing population in the mid-20th Century, when many Puerto Ricans moved to the U.S. mainland for jobs, Puerto Rico's population has grown by 20% in the last two decades, to 4 million people. Similar rates of population growth are expected in the early 21st Century. For more information, see the website: http://www.prb.org.

Public awareness of ecological issues has increased dramatically in Puerto Rico in the last few decades. Examples include the growing popularity of non-consumptive activities, such as scuba diving and tours to nature reserves. You can learn more about how you can help shape Puerto Rico's future by supporting the organizations listed on page 126.

Brown Pelican

How to Use This Book

One way to start using this book is to read the introductory material, and then scan the species accounts and photographs to get a general sense of the layout and species covered. You can later use the index to find species of particular interest. Following this introduction, the endemic species are listed first, followed by the non-endemic species. Within these two groups, individual species appear approximately in the taxonomic sequence of the American Ornithologists' Union, Checklist of North American Birds, 7th edition (http://www.aou.org). This list is designed to position birds that are closely related in adjacent parts of the list, and is used by most other bird books. In the non-endemic bird section, seabirds and birds of marshes and ponds are mostly listed first, while land birds appear later. In general, most of the larger birds appear early in the sequence, while smaller birds appear later. Species accounts have several sections:

NAMES: The English name is listed first, followed by the Latin and Spanish names. Spanish bird names are less standardized than English names. See the Spanish list at the website of the Sociedad Ornitológica Puertorriqueña (page 126).

IDENTIFICATION: A short description of key field marks appears first, followed by the bird's approximate length and weight. The length of the bird is measured from the tip of the bill to the tip of the tail. Since weights and lengths were selected from a variety of sources, a comparison of measurements among species is possible in only a general sense. Also, birds will often look larger or smaller than their weight or length might suggest, depending on the relative proportions of the tail and the body, whether the bird fluffs up its plumage, and many other factors.

HABITAT: Typical habitat in Puerto Rico.

HABITS: Behavior, diet, and nesting are described if space allows, but since priority has been given to the photographs, this information may have been truncated. Where helpful, a description of the common song or call is included, usually using a published example from the Birds of North America monographs, Wetmore, Raffaele, or other authors. Attempts to translate a bird's vocalization into a written description are difficult, but once a bird song is heard, transcriptions are helpful memory devices. Bird banding and breeding bird data were provided by the Patuxent Wildlife Research Center: http://www.pwrc.usgs.gov/bbs/Puerto_Rico/.

STATUS AND CONSERVATION: Species are classified as common, uncommon, rare, accidental (occurring only a few times in any decade), or endangered; also as permanent resident, winter visitor or migrant. The term "winter" is used loosely to mean the period when migrant species that nest in North America or elsewhere reside in Puerto Rico. For many species, that period includes part of the spring and fall as well as winter. Increases or decreases in population are noted, as are threats to the species.

RANGE: Breeding and wintering ranges are summarized. Some subspecies of interest as well as possible taxonomic changes are described, where relevant. For many species, a regular location to find them in Puerto Rico is included.

PHOTOGRAPHS: Over 80 photographers have contributed their work to this effort. They are credited in the acknowledgement section on page 128. Where photos were taken of mist-netted, caged or rehabilitated birds, an asterisk appears next to the photo credit for that photo.

Our CD-ROM contains more text and photos, plus additional species and audio clips. The books by Raffaele listed on page 127 contain more detailed descriptions of plumage and voice, plus dates of nesting and migration.

Puerto Rican Tody

ENDEMIC BIRD SPECIES

Puerto Rican Parrot[†]	13
Puerto Rican Lizard-Cuckoo[††]	14
Puerto Rican Screech-Owl[*]	15
Puerto Rican Nightjar	16
Green Mango	17
Puerto Rican Emerald	18
Puerto Rican Tody	19
Puerto Rican Woodpecker[**]	20
Puerto Rican Flycatcher[*]	21
Puerto Rican Vireo	22
Adelaide's Warbler	23
Elfin-woods Warbler	24
Puerto Rican Tanager	25
Puerto Rican Spindalis	26
Puerto Rican Bullfinch	27
Yellow-shouldered Blackbird	28

POSSIBLE "NEW" ENDEMIC SPECIES

Lesser Antillean Pewee (Puerto Rican Pewee)[†††]	98
Greater Antillean Oriole (Puerto Rican Oriole)[†††]	119

*   Also found on some of the Virgin Islands.
** Formerly found in the Virgin Islands.
†   Formerly found on islands in the eastern Caribbean.
†† Possibly inhabited some of the Virgin Islands.
††† American Ornithologists' Union has not approved these
    taxonomic changes.

Puerto Rican Parrot   *Amazona vittata*   **Cotorra de Puerto Rico**

IDENTIFICATION: A large green parrot with a red forehead and white eye ring. In flight, its wing feathers flash a brilliant blue color. Length: 30-33 cm.; weight: 250-300 g.

HABITAT: Formerly found in all forest habitats in Puerto Rico, Vieques, and Culebra.

HABITS: Travels in pairs or small flocks. It eats the fruits, bark, seeds, flowers or leaves of over 60 plant species. Important food trees currently are the sierra palm (*Prestoea montana*), and to a lesser extent the tabonuco tree (*Dacryodes excelsa*). The parrot makes a variety of squawks and squealing notes, as well as a distinctive bugling call in flight. Its nest is a cavity in a tree trunk, usually the palo colorado tree (*Cyrilla racemiflora*). It has adapted to artificial nest cavities. Two to four eggs are laid from February to May. The female incubates the eggs for 26 days, and the young fledge at about nine weeks of age.

STATUS AND CONSERVATION: Common into the 19th Century, with a population of perhaps a million birds. The wild population declined to 13 birds in 1975, and the species is now an endangered species. Habitat loss, hunting, and the pet trade contributed to the decline. Under aggressive protection, the wild population recovered to 45-47 birds but then dropped to 21-23 birds after Hurricane Hugo in 1989. The population is now about 30 birds in the wild in El Yunque and 220 in captivity at aviaries in El Yunque and Río Abajo. Of the 34 captive-raised parrots released into El Yunque in 2000-2002, 41% survived the first year in the wild. Threats include nest predation by Pearly-eyed Thrashers, Red-tailed Hawks and rats, loss of nest trees and food sources after hurricanes, bot fly infestations of young birds, bees taking over nest cavities, and limited genetic diversity of the population. Conservation measures include improving natural nest cavities by deepening them or adding drainage, or even providing artificial nest cavities. Biologists plan to release additional captive-bred Puerto Rican Parrots in Río Abajo State Forest to establish a second wild population (perhaps late 2006). This would reduce the chances that a single hurricane could wipe out as large a proportion of the population as did Hurricane Hugo.

Range: Currently nests in El Yunque. Occasionally seen from the Río Espíritu Santo overlook on PR 186. Subfossil evidence suggests this species formerly ranged as far east as Antigua.

Puerto Rican Lizard-Cuckoo
Saurothera vieilloti
Pájaro Bobo Mayor

IDENTIFICATION: A large forest bird with a gray breast and rufous belly. It has a red eye ring, a long tail with prominent white spots underneath, and a long, relatively straight bill. Length: 43 cm.; weight: 77-80 g.
HABITAT: Forest thickets, woodlands, and coffee plantations throughout the island.
HABITS: Moves slowly through vines and thickets, foraging in the middle story and upper canopy for prey. It favors Puerto Rico's abundant lizards (perhaps 3/4 of its diet). It also eats large spiders and insects, including cicadas, beetles, stick insects, and caterpillars. It often keeps its body still while it twists its neck at an odd angle to strike at prey. Although this cuckoo is a large, colorful bird, it is often difficult to see because of its slow movements in thick foliage. However, after rains, the bird will sometimes sit out in the open to dry off and preen. The song is a rapid series of "*caw*" notes, commonly described as "*cow cow, kuk krrk*"; and a variety of low-pitched calls. Its nest is a twig platform in a tree or bush and contains 2-3 blue eggs.
STATUS AND CONSERVATION: Common in thickets, forests, limestone hills, and even suburban neighborhoods with dense vegetation.
RANGE: Endemic to Puerto Rico, but possibly inhabited some of the Virgin Islands. Typical locations to find this species are at the beginning of the Granados Trail in Guánica State Forest, on the trails at Guajataca and Vega State Forests, or around the parking lot and entrance road to the El Portal visitor center in El Yunque. Lizard-cuckoos, *Saurothera,* are found only in the Caribbean, with three other species found on other islands: Hispaniola (the Hispaniolan Lizard-Cuckoo, *Saurothera longirostris*); Jamaica (the Jamaican Lizard-Cuckoo, *Saurothera vetula*); and Cuba plus some of the Bahama Islands (Great Lizard-Cuckoo, *Saurothera merlini*).

14

Puerto Rican Screech-Owl   *Megascops nudipes*   **Múcaro Común, Múcaro**

IDENTIFICATION: A small owl with white "eyebrows;" dark brown above and white below, with dark vertical streaking on the breast. The Latin name for the species, *"nudipes,"* refers to the unfeathered legs and feet, unlike most related owls. Length: 23-25 cm.; weight: males 137 g., females 143 g. (See also photos on the front cover and page 4).

HABITAT: Forests, woodlots, tree-filled gardens, and forest edges. It prefers woods with a well-developed understory, plus large hardwood trees or palms for nest cavities.

HABITS: Although vocal throughout the year, this owl can be hard to see since it is nocturnal and often sings while hidden deep within thick foliage. However, the Screech-Owl may be seen briefly as it flies across roads. It can also be seen when hawking insects attracted to lights in wooded areas. Feeds on large insects, and occasionally small birds, lizards, and rodents. Owls swallow small prey whole, and then regurgitate indigestible components in a hard pellet. Unlike most birds, owls have front-facing eyes and binocular vision to aid in capturing prey. When the Screech-Owl is alarmed it will elongate its body and raise short feather tufts that look like "ears" (see photo above). The voice is a low-pitched, trill; from close up, a click can be heard just as the song begins. Also makes a jumble of hoots and cackles that sounds like monkeys. The nest is in a hole in a tree; 1-2 eggs. The home range is 2-5 hectares, smaller than for related owls of similar size.

STATUS AND CONSERVATION: Common in appropriate habitat. Myths persist that owls will bring bad luck or eat coffee beans. However, they are protected by law.

RANGE: Endemic to Puerto Rico and the Virgin Islands. A regular location is along PR 191 above the visitor center in El Yunque.

Puerto Rican Nightjar *Caprimulgus noctitherus* **Guabairo Pequeño de Puerto Rico**

IDENTIFICATION: A mottled, black and brown night bird. The male has white outer tail feathers visible in flight. Length: 22-23 cm.; weight: 39.8-41.3 g.

HABITAT: Coastal dry scrub forests in localized areas of southwestern Puerto Rico.

HABITS: Typically perches on a branch at night and then flies out to catch insects. Like Nighthawks (page 90), the Nightjar has stiff bristles around its wide mouth to aid in localizing airborne insects. The song is a rapid series of "*whip*" notes given from a tree limb. The Nightjar requires forests with a leaf litter layer on the ground for nesting. In fact it really does not make a nest, but places its 1-2 eggs directly on the leaf litter, often under a low bush. The eggs are light brown, with darker brown or purple splotches. If an intruder approaches the nest too closely, the incubating bird will fly directly away from the nest and vibrate its wings to try to attract the potential predator away from the eggs. Such distraction displays are common in ground-nesting birds. The incubation period is 18-20 days. The chicks move to different locations on the ground multiple times before finally starting to fly about 14 days after hatching.

STATUS AND CONSERVATION: The Puerto Rican Nightjar is on the federal endangered species list. It was discovered in the late 19th Century but was then lost to science until rediscovered in 1961. About 800 pairs breed in southwestern Puerto Rico, but the current range probably covers less than 10% of its former range on the island. It probably lived in dry lowland forests and possibly moist limestone hill forests from north-western Puerto Rico, east to Bayamón. Habitat destruction and the introduced mongoose may well have been responsible for eliminating the Nightjar from much of its former range. About half of the current range is protected in the Guánica and Susúa State Forests, but past proposals to place a garbage dump and other developments on public and private lands threaten the bird. In addition, nearby development may create habitat disturbances and make it easier for feral cats to penetrate protected forest areas. Deforestation, fires, road construction, and fire ants are threats, as well as cattle and goat grazing on the private lands where the species occurs.

RANGE: Endemic to Puerto Rico. It has been found recently between Ponce and Lajas at such locations as Guánica and Susúa State Forests, Guayanilla Hills, Parguera Hills, and the Sierra Bermeja. However, the species is far more often heard than seen.

Green Mango
Anthracothorax viridis
Zumbador Verde de Puerto Rico, Colibrí Verde

IDENTIFICATION: A large hummingbird with a curved bill. Both sexes are green above and below, with a bluish tail. The color and intensity depend on the light's angle. Length: 11-12 cm.; weight: 6.6-7.2 g.

HABITAT: Forests, coffee plantations, and forest edges in mountains and foothills.

HABITS: Feeds mainly on insects (such as beetles, flies, lantern flies), spiders, and flower nectar. It sometimes fly-catches insects in mid-air, but more typically gleans insects from leaves and bark. Like the Puerto Rican Emerald, the Mango sometimes "robs" nectar from flowers by piercing them at the base, rather than probing the flower past the stamen. Individual Mangos will aggressively fight off rival hummingbirds from prized food sources, like African tulip trees. The voice is a low-pitched twitter. Hummingbirds can see light in the ultraviolet range of the spectrum which allows them to detect patterns in flowers that are invisible to the human eye. The tiny, cup-shaped nest is made of plant fibers, covered with lichen, typically placed on a tree limb much higher than nests of other hummingbird species in Puerto Rico. The female lays two white eggs. Although the female does all the incubation and caring for the young, the male often stands guard on a neighboring branch while the female incubates.

STATUS AND CONSERVATION: Common in mountain forests where it basically replaces the Antillean Mango of the lowlands.

RANGE: Endemic to Puerto Rico, it is the common large hummingbird in the central and western mountains. Typical sites to find this species are along PR 186 in Caribbean National Forest, the grounds of the parador Hacienda Juanita, near Maricao; Hacienda Gripiñas in Jayuya, and other locations in the central mountains of Puerto Rico.

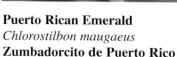

Puerto Rican Emerald
Chlorostilbon maugaeus
Zumbadorcito de Puerto Rico

IDENTIFICATION: The male's body is iridescent green, with a black, forked tail. The lower
bill is flesh-colored or red with a black tip. The
female is light below and has a white-tipped tail.
Length: 9-11 cm.; weight: 2.8-3.6 g.

HABITAT: Forests, mangroves, and gardens.

HABITS: Feeds on insects (lantern flies, mosquitoes, and other fly species), spiders, and nectar. The male often forages higher in the forest
canopy than the female, and is more likely to
feed on nectar. Hummingbirds are very territorial and will mount intense, aerial chases to protect their favorite forest patch. Some Emeralds
will "rob" nectar from flowers, by piercing the
flower at the base. The song is a high-pitched squeal; also utters a sharp, squeaky note when
chasing other hummingbirds. Breeds at any time of year, but especially in February-May
before the beginning of heavy rains. The nest is a tiny cup made of lichens, tree ferns, and other
plant material, and stretches as the two young birds grow. The eggs are tiny: only 8x13 mm.
The nest has been used as a folk remedy for asthma.

STATUS AND CONSERVATION: The common small hummingbird in most of Puerto Rico,
except on the northeast coast, Culebra, and Vieques, where the Antillean Crested
Hummingbird (page 93) replaces it.

RANGE: Endemic to Puerto Rico.

Puerto Rican Tody
Todus mexicanus
San Pedrito de Puerto Rico

IDENTIFICATION: A tiny, brightly-colored forest bird with a short tail, emerald green upperparts, and a bright red throat and lower bill. The sides are washed with yellow. Males have gray eyes, while females have white eyes. Length: 11 cm.; weight: 5-6 g. See also photos on pages 2, 11, 126, and the back cover.

HABITAT: All forest types with dense thickets and vines, as long as there are earthen banks or road cuts for nesting.

HABITS: Sits quietly, with its bill tilted up, as it rapidly scans the forest understory for insect prey. It sits so still that it is often hard to see despite its bright colors. Suddenly it will fly up to grab an insect off the underside of a leaf or branch, and then land on a new perch. Less commonly it catches flying insects. The Tody eats insects, as well as spiders, and occasional small lizards and fruits. The common calls include a click or an insect-like, "*pree*" note. The breeding behavior of the Tody is unusual among Puerto Rican birds. Every year, each pair digs a narrow, 25-35 cm.-long burrow, in an earth bank over an eight-week period, typically between February and May. The female lays 2-4 white eggs. Each egg is equivalent to one quarter of the body weight of the female: more than twice as heavy, proportionately, as in most other bird species. The Tody can lower its body temperature by up to 11 degrees Centigrade to conserve heat during cold weather, especially when breeding. Both sexes incubate the eggs over a period of about 21 days. Sometimes Todies other than the parents assist in incubation and raising the young.

STATUS AND CONSERVATION: A common forest species, but suffers from nest predation by the introduced mongoose. In historical times, humans captured them for food.

RANGE: Endemic to Puerto Rico. Regular locations to find the Puerto Rican Tody are along the trails in El Yunque, Guánica State Forest and other forest reserves. The Tody family, *Todidae,* is endemic to the Greater Antilles. The other four tody species are endemic to other islands: 2 species on Hispaniola and one each on Jamaica and Cuba.

Puerto Rican Woodpecker *Melanerpes portoricensis* Carpintero de Puerto Rico

IDENTIFICATION: Black upper parts, with a bright red throat and breast, and a white forehead. The lower abdomen and flanks are buff-colored. Its white rump patch is striking in flight. The female (upper right photo) has less red below than the male. Length: 23-27 cm.; average weight: about 70 g.
HABITAT: Forests, coffee plantations, mangroves, palm groves, parks and gardens.
HABITS: Gleans insects from bark, and probes or drills holes in tree trunks and limbs for its favorite foods: beetle larvae, ants, earwigs, and other insects. The woodpecker has stiff tail feathers that help the bird brace itself to chisel into wood. It occasionally eats scorpions, lizards, and frogs; 1/4 or more of its diet consists of berries and palm fruits. The smaller female is more likely than the male to forage on smaller branches in the canopy and is more likely to glean insects from plant surfaces or cracks, rather than peck holes for prey. Like other woodpeckers, the Puerto Rican Woodpecker has a barbed tongue and sticky saliva that help it remove insects from crevices and bored holes. The ligaments that control the tongue are so long that they are stored under the skin around the back of the skull. When flying, it gives several bursts of wing flaps, then pauses between wing bursts, producing an undulating flight path. Small groups will chatter in dead or sparsely-leafed trees like *Cecropia*. Calls include a loud series of "*wicka*" notes. Makes a drumming sound by hammering on trees. The Puerto Rican Woodpecker excavates a nest cavity in a tree, or occasionally a utility pole, and lays 4-6 white eggs. Sometimes it nests in loose colonies. The woodpecker can be attracted to backyard suet feeders and will chase off grackles and other birds if they approach its food too closely.
STATUS AND CONSERVATION: Common in forests and woodlots throughout Puerto Rico. Its nest cavities are used by other birds including the endemic Puerto Rican Flycatcher and the endangered Yellow-shouldered Blackbird.
RANGE: Endemic to Puerto Rico and Vieques, formerly in the Virgin Islands. A regular location to find this species is around the parking lot at the El Portal visitor center in El Yunque.

Puerto Rican Flycatcher
Myiarchus antillarum
Juí, Juí de Puerto Rico

IDENTIFICATION: A flycatcher with a dark brown back and light undersides. It has two faint, buff wing bars. Length: 18-20 cm.; weight: 23 g.
HABITAT: Lower elevation forests, especially in coastal scrub forests; coffee plantations.
HABITS: The Puerto Rican Flycatcher is well camouflaged as it sits on branches in the lower and middle level of the forest, waiting to fly out after insects. Prey include flies, weevils, caterpillars, bees, wasps, dragonflies, and hemipteran insects, but about 15% of the diet consists of fruits and berries. Snails, lizards and frogs are occasionally eaten. Flycatchers' jaws have ligaments that reflexively snap shut when the bird grabs an insect in mid-air. The common song is a waning whistle, reflected in its common name in Spanish, "*Juí.*" It calls frequently throughout the day in the breeding season. Like many other flycatcher species, the Puerto Rican Flycatcher has a more complicated, beautiful "dawn song" that it gives early in the day. It nests from February to July in a tree cavity or artificial nest box. Clutches range from 3-6 yellowish eggs with brown spots. Both the male and female incubate the eggs. Unlike many other landbirds, the male develops a brood patch just like the female (the brood patch is an area of reduced or absent feathers on the belly to efficiently transfer heat while incubating eggs). Young fledge about 15-16 days after hatching.
STATUS AND CONSERVATION: Common, but sometimes hard to see outside the breeding season when it is less vocal. After a major hurricane in 1928, the population dropped dramatically. It was not recorded from the Virgin Islands until the mid-20th Century, but it is not clear whether the "range expansion" there might reflect a re-colonization after native forests recovered from centuries of intensive sugarcane farming. Biaggi relates that campesinos believed the Puerto Rican Flycatcher delivered warnings of good or bad occurrences.
RANGE: Endemic to Puerto Rico and the Virgin Islands. Regular locations to find this species include Boquerón, Vega, and Guánica state forests. This species was formerly lumped by taxonomists with the Stolid Flycatcher of Jamaica and Hispaniola (*Myiarchus stolidus*), and the LaSagra's Flycatcher (*Myiarchus sagrae*) of Cuba and the Bahamas.

Puerto Rican Vireo
Vireo latimeri
Bien-te-veo

IDENTIFICATION: A small forest bird with a thick bill, a gray head, white breast and light yellow belly. There is a white crescent above and below the eye. Length: 12 cm.; weight: 11-12 g.

HABITAT: Mountain forests, coffee plantations, coastal karst and thorn forests with vine tangles.

HABITS: Carefully searches through foliage for insect prey such as caterpillars, grasshoppers, cicadas, beetles, and aphids. It also eats spiders, lizards and small berries. It prefers mid- to lower levels of trees, but because it forages slowly in thick vegetation and vine tangles, the bird may be difficult to locate despite its loud voice. The song is reflected in its Spanish name: "*bien-te-veo*." Its nest is a cup on a tree limb and contains three pinkish eggs with brown spots.

STATUS AND CONSERVATION: This bird is still common, especially in thorn forests of the southwest and in the limestone hills. However, between 1973 and 1996, it steadily declined in Guánica State Forest and possibly elsewhere, most likely due to nest predation, and to nest parasitism by the Shiny Cowbird (*Molothrus bonariensis*, page 118).

RANGE: Endemic to Puerto Rico, where it occurs in the western two thirds of the island, less commonly in El Yunque. Regular locations to find this species are in Guánica State Forest and at the picnic area at Km 16.2 in Maricao State Forest.

Adelaide's Warbler
Dendroica adelaidae
Reinita Mariposera

IDENTIFICATION: A small warbler with a blue-gray back, and a yellow breast and throat. It has a yellow and white line above the eye, and a white or yellow crescent below the eye. Length: 12 cm.; weight: 7 g. The species was named after Adelaide Swift, the daughter of Robert Swift, who collected the initial ("type") specimen for the Smithsonian Institution. Some other bird species are named after friends or relatives of collectors and taxonomists, or their financial sponsors.

HABITAT: Dry, lowland forests and some moist forests, with tangles of vines and thickets, especially in the southwest and the northern limestone hills.

HABITS: Adelaide's Warbler gleans insects at middle and higher levels of the forest. Prey includes caterpillars, lantern flies, grasshoppers, weevils, other beetles, stink bugs, flies, spiders, and rarely small frogs. It often travels in mixed species flocks, including todies, vireos, and migrant warblers. The call is a sharp, loud "*chik*", and the song is a sudden, ascending or descending trill. It sings energetically into late morning, when most other birds have quieted down, and often sings at any time of year. Its nest is a cup placed 3-20 feet high in a tree or shrub, and contains 2-4 white eggs with brown spots.

RANGE: Endemic to Puerto Rico and Vieques. Typical locations to find this bird in Puerto Rico are at Guánica and Vega State Forests and on the trails near the visitor center at Cabo Rojo National Wildlife Refuge.

TAXONOMY: PASSERIFORMES; PARULIDAE. The Adelaide's Warbler was formerly lumped with related species on Barbuda and St. Lucia. Those islands are 210 and 350 miles, respectively, from Puerto Rico. Taxonomists recently split the complex into three species based on variations in plumage and song. Genetic studies suggest that the populations on the three islands have been separated from each other for many millenia. The other islands' species are now called the Barbuda Warbler *(Dendroica subita)* and the St. Lucia Warbler *(Dendroica delicata)*.

Elfin-woods Warbler
Dendroica angelae
Reinita de Bosque Enano

IDENTIFICATION: This warbler is black above, with a large black "cheek" patch, white facial markings and two white wing bars. The underparts are white, with black streaks from the throat to the belly. The black tail has white spots on the underside. The bill is longer and the wings more rounded than in many species of migratory warblers from North America, a general pattern among Caribbean endemic warblers known as the "island phenomenon." Length: 12 cm.; weight: 8.4 g.

HABITAT: Mountain cloud forest and lower montane forest from 370-1,030 meters elevation.

HABITS: This warbler is often seen only briefly as it rapidly gleans insects from branches and leaves, rarely staying in one location for more than a few seconds. It sometimes hovers to glean an insect off a leaf, or rarely catches an insect in mid-air. In dwarf forest it forages just below the canopy, often in tangles of vines. In taller forest, it prefers middle levels of the forest. It often travels in mixed-species flocks including Lesser Antillean Pewee (Puerto Rican Pewee), American Redstart, and Puerto Rican Tanager. The song is a galloping series of dry, tick notes. The call is a sharp, buzzy note. Both sexes make a cup nest in a tangle of vines or clump of leaves in the canopy, sometimes with a *Cecropia* leaf as protective cover. Two or three eggs are laid in April. Because of its restricted range, dense habitat, and superficial resemblance to the migratory Black-and-white Warbler, this endemic species was not discovered until May 1972. Drs. Cameron and Angela Kepler were working in the El Yunque forest on other species when they discovered the Elfin-woods Warbler.

STATUS AND CONSERVATION: Currently a rare permanent resident that was initially thought to be restricted to high altitude, dwarf forests. But it was subsequently found to be commoner in taller forest, at slightly lower elevations. This suggests that it may have been more widespread, but survived on high ridges during Puerto Rico's bottleneck of deforestation in the early 20th Century. Although the warbler's habitat is occasionally threatened by the construction of communications antennae and roads, most of its habitat is in protected public forests. Hurricanes periodically defoliate trees at high elevation, but both the forest ecosystem and the warbler have adapted to these storms.

RANGE: Endemic to Puerto Rico, this species is found in higher forests and ridges in the Sierra de Luquillo, Caribbean National Forest (El Yunque), Sierra de Cayey, and the Cordillera Central at Toro Negro and Maricao State Forests. A regular location to find this species is in the forest adjacent to the picnic area at KM 16.2 on PR 120 near Maricao. Three related species of warblers are endemic to other Caribbean islands: the Arrow-headed Warbler of Jamaica (*Dendroica pharetra*), the Plumbeous Warbler of Guadeloupe and Dominica (*Dendroica plumbea*), and the Whistling Warbler of St. Vincent (*Catharopeza bishopi*).

Puerto Rican Tanager
Nesospingus speculiferus
Llorosa,
Llorosa de Puerto Rico

IDENTIFICATION: This forest bird has an olive-brown back, darker on top of the head. Its underparts are white, with light gray streaking, and it has a small, white wing patch. Immature birds lack the wing patch and have darker undersides. Length: 16-20 cm.; weight: 35-36 g.

HABITAT: Mountain forests, coffee plantations, and gardens at higher elevations.

HABITS: The Puerto Rican Tanager travels in pairs or small flocks rapidly foraging in bushes and trees for insects (moths, caterpillars, beetles, grasshoppers, ants), spiders, snails, and lizards. About 40% of the diet in one study was fruit and some seeds. The tanager is quite active, but often difficult to see in thick vegetation. The tanager roosts at night in large noisy flocks in bamboo or palm trees. It has been observed "anting," a behavior in many species in which a bird will rub ants on its feathers and skin, or allow ants to crawl over its body. Birds are presumed "to ant" to take advantage of formic acid or other ant secretions to kill parasites, fungi, or bacteria on the birds'

feathers or skin. Mixed-species flocks in Puerto Rico average 5-6 species of birds, with the Puerto Rican Tanager often being an important ringleader. The tanager uses unique call notes to communicate with other species in the flock. It defends a territory during the breeding season from January to July. It builds its cup-shaped nest in a vine tangle far out on a tree limb, about 2-10 meters above the ground. The nest is made of leaves, roots, vines and strands of fungus, lined with strips of palm leaves, and contains 2-3 white or cream-colored eggs with brown spots.

STATUS AND CONSERVATION: This bird belongs to an endemic genus found only on Puerto Rico. In fact, *Nesospingus* is the only bird genus endemic to Puerto Rico. The Puerto Rican Tanager is common at higher elevations. In the early 20th Century it was restricted to mountain ranges at just a few locations such as Maricao, Toro Negro, and Carite State Forests; Caribbean National Forest (El Yunque), and near Cidra. This spotty distribution was perhaps related to the almost total deforestation of Puerto Rico in the late 19th Century, and reflected the few refugia where isolated populations survived a century ago in coffee plantations or high ridgetop forest fragments. More recently this species has expanded into other suitable habitat such as near Comerío, Aibonito, Barranquitas, Adjuntas and the haystack hills in Ciales.

RANGE: Endemic to Puerto Rico. Regular locations to find this species are around Parador Hacienda Juanita near Maricao, or along PR 191 above the El Portal visitor center in El Yunque.

Puerto Rican Spindalis
Spindalis portoricensis
Reina Mora

IDENTIFICATION: The male is green above with an orange neck and breast. The head is black, with white stripes. The dark wings have a diffuse white wing bar. The female is dull olive green, with fuzzy gray streaking below, and a vague suggestion of the male's white stripe-pattern on the head (photo at right). Length: 17 cm.; weight: 26-31 g.
HABITAT: Forests, gardens, and plantations with fruiting plants.
HABITS: This tanager travels in pairs or small flocks at all levels

in forests and plantations. It primarily eats berries and fruits such as figs, blackberries and *Cecropia* fruits, but will consume some insects. This species persistently sings a squeaky series of notes from a canopy branch or sometimes while circling over a favorite perch. The call is a weak "*tseet*." Like many other species, the male will sometimes confuse its own reflection with a rival bird and will repeatedly attack windows and mirrors to drive off the "intruder." Its nest ranges from a small cup, to bulky, deeper nests. It lays 2-4 light blue eggs with brown speckling.
RANGE: Endemic to Puerto Rico. Can be found in forested areas such as El Yunque or near Maricao. See also photos on pages 9, 126 and front cover.
TAXONOMY: PASSERIFORMES; THRAUPIDAE. Formerly called the Stripe-headed Tanager (*Spindalis zena*), but taxonomists recently split the Stripe-headed Tanager into four separate species: Puerto Rican Spindalis (*Spindalis portoricensis*), Jamaican Spindalis (*Spindalis nigricephala*), Hispaniolan Spindalis (*Spindalis dominicensis*), and Western Spindalis (*Spindalis zena*) of the Bahamas, Cuba and coastal Mexico.

Puerto Rican Bullfinch *Loxigilla portoricensis* **Comeñame**

IDENTIFICATION: A thick-billed, black, forest bird with large reddish patches above the eyes, on the throat, and under the base of the tail. The female is slightly smaller and duller colored than the male. Length: 17-19 cm.; weight: 32-33 g.

HABITAT: Moist and dry forests with thick undergrowth, thick brushy areas, and coffee plantations throughout the island, except the far eastern end.

HABITS: Feeds on seeds, fruits, and buds in dense vegetation at any level in the forest, but mostly at middle levels in moist forest, and in the canopy of dry and elfin forests. It will stay on one perch and carefully inspect its immediate surroundings for food before moving on to the next perch. It sometimes leans off a branch until it is almost hanging, in order to reach an attractive cluster of fruit. Insects (caterpillars, weevils, other beetles), snails, and spiders made up about 1/3 of the diet in one study. The song is a series of rich, whistled notes followed by a high-pitched trill. The Bullfinch often sings at any time of day while hidden in treetop vegetation. It also has a low "*tsweet*" note. It makes a globular nest with a side entrance. A typical clutch contains three light green, spotted eggs.

STATUS AND CONSERVATION: Common, but it is more often heard than seen. A slightly larger species (*Loxigilla grandis*), 170 miles to the east on St. Kitts, may be extinct.

RANGE: Endemic to Puerto Rico. Regular in woodlands throughout the island, such as at El Yunque and at Vega, Carite, Guajataca, Maricao and Guánica State Forests. The **Lesser Antillean Bullfinch** (*Loxigilla noctis,* photos below) of the eastern Caribbean has been expanding its range westward and is now common in the Virgin Islands. It is smaller, with a reddish-orange throat patch and eyebrow. Female and immature are brown above and gray below. Length: 14-15 cm.; weight 17 g.

Lesser Antillean Bullfinch

Lesser Antillean Bullfinch

Yellow-shouldered Blackbird
Agelaius xanthomus
Mariquita de Puerto Rico

IDENTIFICATION: Black bird with a yellow "shoulder" patch, and a pointed bill. Unlike many blackbirds, the male and female have similar plumages. The race on Mona Island (*Agelaius xanthomus monensis*) has paler wing patches than the race on the main island of Puerto Rico (*Agelaius xanthomus xanthomus*). Length: 20-23 cm.; weight: males 41 g., females 35 g.

HABITAT: The Yellow-shouldered Blackbird was formerly found in lowlands around Puerto Rico, but is now basically restricted to Mona Island, Roosevelt Roads, and the open, dry forests and mangroves of southwestern Puerto Rico. In the non-breeding season it flocks to fields and livestock corals.

HABITS: Feeds mostly on insects in trees. Prey includes weevils, other beetles, caterpillars, moths, crickets, earwigs, wasps, flies, spiders, occasional snails, and seeds. It sometimes flocks with Greater Antillean Grackles and Shiny Cowbirds, and will fly large distances from roosting or breeding areas to feeding sites. It can be attracted to seed feeders. Pairs are monogamous and display in the nesting season with wing flapping and displaying the wing patches while singing. It nests in colonies and places its cup nest in mangroves, palms, and other trees, or a tree cavity or nest box. On Mona Island, it also uses cliffs for nesting and roosting. The female lays 1-4 greenish or blue eggs with brown spots. She incubates them for 13 days. Both sexes feed the young which leave the nest 13-16 days after hatching.

STATUS AND CONSERVATION: The Yellow-shouldered Blackbird was common in the early 20th Century, but is now on the federal endangered species list. Since the arrival of the Shiny Cowbird from South America in the mid-20th Century, almost all Blackbirds' nests were parasitized by this species, except on Mona Island. Cowbird chicks grow faster than Blackbird chicks and out-compete them for food. Blackbirds are only half as likely to fledge young from nests that are parasitized by cowbirds, compared to nests without cowbirds. In addition, nest predation by rats and Pearly-eyed Thrashers is a problem, as is competition with Caribbean Martins for nest boxes and cavities. The Blackbird's estimated population on the main island of Puerto Rico dropped to only 200-300 in the 1970s, but has since climbed back to about 800 thanks to programs to control cowbirds in southwestern Puerto Rico. The August 2002 post-nesting census in three key areas of southwestern Puerto Rico had 648 blackbirds. In one study, 100% of nests in 1975 had cowbird eggs on the main island of Puerto Rico, compared to only 4.8% of 229 active blackbird nests in 1995. Blackbirds readily accept artificial nest boxes. However, cowbird trapping and control will probably have to be continued indefinitely in order to guarantee the survival of the Yellow-shouldered Blackbird. A fluctuating population of 400-900 survive in the non-threatened subspecies on Mona and Monito Islands, where cowbirds do not occur. Most Yellow-shouldered Blackbirds on Puerto Rico have been banded with an aluminum identification leg band, and many have colored plastic bands that identify their birth year.

RANGE: Endemic to Puerto Rico, Monito, and Mona Islands. Regular in mangroves in southwestern Puerto Rico and at Roosevelt Roads, e.g. on the grounds of the Parador Villa Parguera. At dawn and dusk, small flocks can be seen flying from mangrove roosts past the waterfront in La Parguera or Pitaya.

NON-ENDEMIC BIRD SPECIES

Pied-billed Grebe   *Podilymbus podiceps*   Zaramago

IDENTIFICATION: In breeding plumage the Pied-billed Grebe has a dark body, dark eye, and a white bill with a black stripe across it. When not in breeding plumage, the bill is plain gray or yellowish, without the black stripe. Length: 30-38 cm.; weight: 253-568 g.
HABITAT: Ponds, marshes, and canals.
HABITS: Dives for small fish, crustaceans, and insect larvae. It also dives to escape danger, and can resurface a surprising distance away. Swallows some of its own feathers and creates a feather ball in the stomach, which is presumed to protect the stomach lining from fish bones. The nest is a mat of decaying vegetation and contains 5-6 eggs. Chicks often hitch a ride on a parent's back, sometimes even when the parent dives.
STATUS AND CONSERVATION: A common, permanent resident, freshwater bird in Puerto Rico. Protection of wetlands is essential for the species' survival.
RANGE: Nests from southern Canada through Central America and the Caribbean to southern South America. Typical locations in Puerto Rico are the marshes at the Humacao wildlife reserve and the ponds at Dorado and Riomar.

Least Grebe
Tachybaptus dominicus
Tigua
A small, diving bird with a thin, dark bill, a dark body, and a yellow eye. Length: 21-26 cm; weight: 116-133 g. Forages in freshwater ponds, canals, and temporary pools with thick floating vegetation. Dives for aquatic beetles, dragonfly larvae, waterbugs, and other insects, plus crustaceans, tadpoles and small fish. Grebes' feet are set so far back on the body that they cannot walk upright. An uncommon permanent resident, found locally in lowland Puerto Rico. Drainage of wetlands in the last century has destroyed much habitat for both grebe species. Regular in the ponds north of Caño Tiburones Nature Reserve.

White-tailed Tropicbird
Phaethon lepturus
Chirre

IDENTIFICATION: A white, tern-like seabird with black wing tips and a black bar across the top of each wing. The two white central tail feathers are narrow and very long. A black line extends through the eye. The bill is yellow, orange or reddish-orange. Length: 70-82 cm. (mostly the long tail streamer); weight: 220-410 g.

HABITAT: Nests on isolated rocky cliffs, but spends much of its life far out at sea.

HABITS: Often flies with rapid, deep wing beats high over the ocean, but will hover like an apparition over a fishing boat, unnoticed by human mariners until someone happens to look straight overhead. One theory is that the tropicbird has learned to home in on boats to catch flying fish that boats might flush. When it lands at sea, it holds its two central tail feathers high in an arc. The tropicbird travels alone over great distances to feed in patches of warm sea water. It eats squid and small fish—especially flying fish (*Exocoetidae*)—by diving from high above the sea surface. Air sacs in the bird's upper body cushion the impact with the water. Fish species from 14 families of fish have been identified as tropicbird prey in Puerto Rico. It nests on a bare ledge or in a crevice on a rocky cliff or talus slope. Between January and June the female lays a single white or pinkish egg with brown spots. Because this species feeds far at sea, each parent may incubate for 7-9 days straight before being relieved by the other parent. The adult may lose 20% of its body weight during each incubation shift. The incubation period is long—41 days—and chicks don't fledge until 71-73 days after hatching.

STATUS AND CONSERVATION: A locally common species in late winter and spring near its nesting cliffs. Formerly hunted for food by Native Americans, and later commercially for its feathers. Rats and crabs take a toll of young and eggs. Puerto Rico's population has declined dramatically in recent centuries. It formerly nested on cliffs of the southwestern and northern coasts of the main island of Puerto Rico, but is now restricted to the northwestern coast and Mona, Monito, Culebra, and Cajà de Muerto Islands. Only 2,500-3,500 pairs are estimated to nest in the West Indies.

RANGE: Found in tropical seas around the world. Regular locations to see this species from the main island are the cliffs between Isabela and Barceloneta, especially near Guajataca.

Red-billed Tropicbird
Phaethon aethereus
Chirre de Pico Colorado

A white seabird with a bright red bill, black wing tips and fine black barring on its back and the upperside of each wing. A black line extends through the eye. The two white central tail feathers are narrow and very long. Immature birds lack the long tail. Length: 90-105 cm., most of which is the long tail streamer; weight: 700 g. Similar in behavior and nesting habits to the White-Tailed Tropicbird. Uncommon off its nesting cliffs near Culebra. The total Caribbean population may number 1,800-2,500 breeding pairs, a major decline in the last few centuries. Rats and cats are a threat at some nesting colonies, and egg collecting by humans was formerly a threat.

Wilson's Storm-Petrel
Oceanites oceanicus
Pamperito de Rabo Cuadrado, Golondrina de Mar

A small, dark brown seabird with a prominent white rump patch. Length: 15-19 cm.; weight: 34-35 g. One of the Spanish names for this species is "sea swallow"—a very appropriate name. Like a swallow, the Storm-Petrel rapidly darts back and forth across the ocean in search of food close to the surface. It often faces into the wind, holds its wings in a "V", dangling its legs, and seeming to walk on water. It travels in flocks, and feeds on small marine crustaceans (especially krill), squid, other invertebrates, and fish. A rare species in the Caribbean in late spring, as it migrates from Antarctic breeding islands to cold, productive waters of the North Atlantic. But it may be commoner than reported, since few birders spend much time on the open oceans of the West Indies. Its worldwide population numbers several million breeding pairs.

Audubon's Shearwater
Puffinus lherminieri
Pampero de Audubon

A medium-sized seabird, dark brown above, and white below, with a long, hooked bill. Length: 27-33 cm.; weight: 150-230 g.; Wingspan: 64-74 cm. Shearwaters' long wings allow them to maneuver in light ocean breezes. Catches fish, squid and other crustaceans by grabbing prey near the surface, or chasing prey underwater (pursuit diving). Nests on islands off Culebra, but uncommon even during the breeding season. The West Indian breeding population is only 3,000-5,000 pairs.

Masked Booby
Sula dactylatra
Boba de Cara Azul

IDENTIFICATION: Largest booby; white seabird with a yellow bill, black tail, black trailing edge to the wings, and black skin around the bill (the "Mask"). Length: 74-86 cm.; weight: 1,200-2,300 g., females being larger than males.
HABITAT: Feeds for long periods at sea in warm tropical waters.
HABITS: Forages in deeper waters than other booby species, and usually hunts alone. It dives from a height of up to 30 meters into the top 3-4 meters of the sea after fish (especially flying fish (*Exocoetidae*), and jacks (*Carangidae*)) and some squid. During the breeding season in February-August, just before mating, the male displays to the female by slowly parading around her, displaying his feet, and offering feathers or pebbles. Other mating displays include "sky pointing" (stretching the neck and holding the head straight up for several seconds). Like other booby species, males make a high-pitched whistle, and females a honking sound. The booby nests on the ground on rocky islands, and lays one or two white eggs. Both sexes take turns incubating the eggs over a 38-49 day period. Boobies, like pelicans, do not have a brood patch: an area of exposed skin on the belly that warms the egg during the incubation period. Instead boobies wrap their feet over the eggs to incubate them. As with other booby species, one chick may kill the other chick. Both parents feed the chicks. The young fly about four months after hatching.
STATUS AND CONSERVATION: An uncommon seabird, but found close to nesting colonies near Culebra and Monito Islands. Only 550-650 pairs are estimated to breed in the Caribbean.
RANGE: Occurs throughout the world's tropical oceans.

Red-footed Booby
Sula sula
Boba Blanca

IDENTIFICATION: Smallest booby; white seabird with dark trailing edges to the wings, and bright red feet. Some individuals are brown, but the tail is white. Length: 69-79 cm.; weight: 850-1,100 g., the females being larger.
HABITAT: Feeds for long periods at sea in deep tropical oceans.
HABITS: Flies great distances in search of food, and will dive from a height of 4-8 meters as it hunts squid and fish (especially flying fish). It often feeds with other seabirds over schools of tuna and other predatory fish as they force smaller prey to the surface. Does not start breeding until 3-4 years of age. Both sexes incubate one egg for 45-46 days.
STATUS AND CONSERVATION: A local seabird, not commonly seen because if forages far out to sea. However, large colonies are found at Mona and Monito, as well as smaller numbers near Culebra and the Virgin Islands. Introduced predators may decimate colonies, such as monkeys did on Desecheo Island. The West Indian breeding population is only 8,200-10,000 pairs.
RANGE: Occurs throughout the world's tropical oceans.

Brown Booby
Sula leucogaster
**Boba Prieta,
Boba Parda**

IDENTIFICATION: A large brown seabird with a white belly and underwing, and a yellowish bill. The immature plumage has duller gray undersides; this plumage is kept for the first two years. Length: 64-85 cm.; weight: 950-1,800 g.
HABITAT: Feeds at sea, often relatively close to shore.
HABITS: Feeds by flying over the ocean looking for schools of fish or squid, and then diving like a dart, with its wings streamlined against its body. It especially favors flying fish---and sometimes squid close to the surface. Unlike most birds, boobies do not have nostrils---an adaptation to the intense impact of diving from great heights. The booby uses its wings and feet to propel itself underwater. Occasionally young boobies perch on the railing or lines of a boat and allow sailors to approach them closely. The booby nests on the ground on rocky islands, where it incubates one or two white eggs. The older booby chick often kills the younger chick, a behavior called siblicide, a form of brood reduction.
STATUS AND CONSERVATION: Common just off the coast, especially in far eastern and far western Puerto Rico, closer to its nesting colonies. Many of these colonies are now designated as wildlife refuges, to protect them from human disturbance and predation by rats, cats and other predators. Formerly, nesting colonies were raided by commercial egg collectors. Monkeys introduced to Desecheo Island eliminated most breeding seabirds there. Oil spills and entanglement with fishing nets are still threats. Only 5,500-7,800 pairs are estimated to breed in the West Indies.
RANGE: The Brown Booby occurs throughout the world's tropical oceans. In Puerto Rico the most reliable area to see this species from shore is at the Rincón and Cabo Rojo lighthouses, close to nesting colonies on Monito Island in the Mona Passage. The largest colonies in Puerto Rico are found within the Cordillera Natural Reserve (between Fajardo and Culebra). Thus this species is regularly seen from the ferries to Culebra and Vieques Islands.

34

Brown Pelican   *Pelecanus occidentalis*   **Pelícano Pardo, Alcatraz**

IDENTIFICATION: A familiar, large brown seabird with a white head, a long bill, and a huge, expandable throat pouch. Adults in breeding plumage have a chestnut neck and yellow feathers on the head as well. Immature birds (see photo at right) are dull brown with white underparts for the first three years. Length: 100-137 cm.; weight: 3,500 g. See also photos on pages 8 and 10.

HABITAT: Feeds in shallow lagoons, reef edges, and bays, sometimes at the edge of the surf.

HABITS: Flies singly or in small flocks, sometimes almost touching the ocean surface to take advantage of the "ground effect" i.e., increased lift from the cushion of air that forms under the wing near a flat surface. It hunts for schools of small fish or shrimp, and suddenly dives straight down to capture a school in its huge throat pouch. It then tilts its head back and drains the water out before dining. Frigatebirds and Laughing Gulls sometimes steal its catch. Although the pelican is generally cautious about humans' approach, sometimes it boldly lands on a dock or even in a swimming pool! It breeds throughout the year with peak nesting activity from April to June and from November to January. It builds a large stick nest usually in traditional colonies on offshore islands. It lays 2-4 white eggs. Both sexes incubate the eggs over 28-30 days, and the young can fly 10-12 weeks after hatching. Females don't start breeding until 3 years old.

STATUS AND CONSERVATION: The Brown Pelican is on the federal endangered species list, but is frequently seen feeding in coastal areas. Its nesting success declined due to egg damage from the insecticide DDT, but has recovered with the ban on that insecticide. The population in Puerto Rico experiences low fledging success and major die-offs, primarily of juvenile pelicans. This phenomenon is not well understood. Nesting colonies are susceptible to disturbance by human visitors and nest predators. The Caribbean population numbers 1,500 nesting pairs, but migrants from North America also winter in the West Indies.

RANGE: Inhabits warmer coastal waters throughout the Western Hemisphere. Near Puerto Rico it nests at only a few locations such as Cayo Conejo off Vieques, but can be seen in any coastal area and many salt and freshwater lagoons and lakes.

Magnificent Frigatebird
Fregata magnificens
Tijerilla, Fragata, Tijereta, Rabijunco

IDENTIFICATION: The frigatebird is distinguished by its large size, long, forked tail and long, narrow wings. The male is black with greenish iridescence on the back. It has a red throat sack that it inflates in courtship displays. The female (see photo at left) has a white breast and less iridescence, while the immature bird has an entirely white head—a plumage retained for the first 4-6 years of life (see photo on page 6). The wingspan is 217-244 cm.—by far the longest wingspan of any West Indian bird. Length: 89-114 cm.; weight: 1,000-1,900 g. (only about 5% of the body weight is bone, the lowest percentage of any bird in the world). See also photos on pages 4, 6, and the back cover.
HABITAT: Feeds in lagoons and at sea.
HABITS: The frigatebird can soar at up to 50 km/hour or hover motionless over the ocean areas---a familiar sight throughout coastal Puerto Rico. It feeds by swooping to the ocean surface quickly and snatching a flying fish, other fish species, jellyfish or squid with its 10-cm. long bill. The frigatebird is a "kleptoparasite": it steals much of its food from other birds, such as gulls, terns, pelicans, tropicbirds, boobies, or other frigatebirds. It startles or chases its victim until it forces the victim to drop or regurgitate its catch. The frigatebird then intercepts the falling food in mid-air. The frigatebird does not swim, in part because it has trouble taking off without a strong wind. In addition, the oil gland at the base of the tail is proportionately small compared to other birds, so it cannot waterproof its feathers sufficiently to tolerate prolonged submersion. Unlike many other seabirds, it often returns from the sea to mangrove islands to roost at night. It occasionally soars inland in Puerto Rico, leading to a local expression: "Frigatebird over land; storm at sea." The species has been found hundreds of miles from the ocean in North America after hurricanes. It builds a stick nest in bushes or directly on the ground on protected offshore islands. The single, white egg is incubated for 40-50 days, and the adults care for the young for seven months or more. The young use their bills like swords to fence with neighboring chicks.
STATUS AND CONSERVATION: Common in coastal Puerto Rico. Nesting colonies are susceptible to disturbance by human visitors and nest predators. Throughout the Caribbean, frigatebird populations have declined dramatically in the last few centuries. The Caribbean nesting population is estimated at 4,300-5,300 pairs in 25 colonies. The frigatebird formerly nested on a number of isolated islands around Puerto Rico.
RANGE: Inhabits warmer coastal waters throughout the Western Hemisphere, and also the Cape Verde Islands off West Africa. In Puerto Rico it nests on Monito Island, but can be seen foraging along most coastal areas. San Juan Harbor, especially on the Cataño side, is a regular location.

Great Blue Heron
Ardea herodias
Garzón Cenizo

IDENTIFICATION: The tallest bird in Puerto Rico, the Great Blue Heron has a huge, pointed bill, a gray and blue-gray body, with a black and white head pattern. The "thighs" are chestnut. In flight the Great Blue Heron's long legs trail behind it, and it holds its neck in an "S"-shaped curve. Its slow, deep wing beat is distinctive even at a distance. An all-white form, the Great White Heron, has rarely been sighted in Puerto Rico. Length: 117 cm.; weight: 2,200 g.; wingspan: 183 cm.

HABITAT: Forages on ocean shores, lagoons, rivers, marshes, mangroves, ponds, and occasionally in grassy fields.

HABITS: Feeds mostly on fish, but also will eat amphibians, snakes, crabs and other invertebrates, as well as small mammals and birds when it can catch them. The Great Blue Heron stands motionless for long periods, then quickly grabs a passing fish. It sometimes tosses its prey in the air and then swallows it head first. As with other herons, its middle toe is modified as a comb to preen the feathers on its head and neck. The Great Blue Heron nests in North America in swamp colonies where it builds a stick nest in treetops. Both sexes build the nest, incubate the 2-6 eggs and feed the young. The incubation period is about 27 days, and the young start to fly 51-81 days after hatching.

STATUS AND CONSERVATION: Common winter visitor to Puerto Rico, with a few individuals lingering through the summer and even breeding. Has suffered from hunting, as well as wetland drainage and chemical contamination.

RANGE: Breeds from southern North America to southern Mexico, as well as the Bahamas, the Virgin Islands, Cuba, and the Galapagos Islands. Some birds migrate to winter grounds throughout the Caribbean and Central America, and south to northwestern South America. A regular sight in Puerto Rican lagoons in winter, even next to the busy runway at the San Juan airport.

Great Egret
Ardea alba
Garza Real

IDENTIFICATION: A large white heron, with a long, yellow bill, and dark legs. In flight it usually curls its long neck in an "S" shape. Formerly called Common Egret, American Egret, and Great White Egret. Length: 80-104 cm.; weight: 700-1,500 g.
HABITAT: Fresh and salt water ponds, canals, mangroves, lagoons, moist grassy fields, even small urban streams.
HABITS: Usually forages alone, either walking slowly or waiting for its prey to approach. It feeds on fish, typically less than 12 cm. long, and also on frogs, insects, crustaceans, and sometimes small birds. It defends a feeding territory against other egrets and herons. Both sexes build a stick nest in a treetop colony over water. In courtship displays, a pair will stretch their necks, and clack their bills. The female lays 3-5 eggs. Incubation lasts 25-26 days, and the chicks fledge at about six weeks. Birds breeding in the eastern USA winter in the southern USA and the Caribbean. Great Egrets banded in New Jersey and Maryland have been recovered in Puerto Rico.

STATUS AND CONSERVATION: Common, permanent resident of Puerto Rico, with the population increasing in winter as migrants arrive from North America. This species was hunted for its feathers a century ago---like many other egrets and herons---but a public outcry led to an end to the hunting---one of the early successes of the conservation movement. More recently, its breeding success suffered from DDT exposure, but has recovered since that insecticide was banned. Wetlands destruction and pollution have decreased habitat for this species.
RANGE: Breeds in eastern North America south through the Caribbean and Central America to central Argentina. It is also found widely in Africa, Asia and Australia.

Greater Flamingo
Phoenicopterus ruber
Flamenco

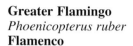

A long-legged, pink bird with a dramatically curved, black-tipped bill. The feather color derives from carotenoid pigments found in crustaceans that the bird eats. Length: 120-145 cm.; weight: 2,100-4,100 g. Nested at salt flats in Puerto Rico, but was eliminated by egg collecting, hunting, and disturbance at colonies. Occasional individuals still visit Cabo Rojo from colonies on other islands. May soon be renamed Caribbean Flamingo and split from the Old World form.

38

Snowy Egret
Egretta thula
Garza Blanca

IDENTIFICATION: A white heron with black legs and bill, and yellow feet. The skin at the base of the bill is yellow (orange in breeding season). Immature birds have variable amounts of yellow-green color on the legs. Length: 56-66 cm.; weight: 370 g.
HABITAT: Lagoons, rivers, marshes, mangroves and ponds.
HABITS: Feeds on small fish, amphibians, snakes, crabs, insects, and other invertebrates. It uses its yellow feet to stir up mud and startle its prey, which it grabs with a quick dart of its long bill. Like other egrets, it often flashes its wings open to startle or herd its prey. Its voice is a low-pitched squawk. The Snowy Egret nests in colonies, often with other heron species, in swamps and mangrove islands. The nest is made of sticks and contains 3-5 blue-green eggs. After the breeding season, the Snowy Egret wanders more widely inland away from the coast. In winter the resident Snowy Egret population increases with northern migrants. One Snowy Egret banded in Connecticut was recovered in Puerto Rico.
STATUS AND CONSERVATION: Common, permanent resident of Puerto Rico. In the late Nineteenth Century, the elaborate feathers in the breeding plumage were used in women's hats. The Snowy Egret was in danger of extinction due to hunting pressure. As late as 1910, plumes were sold in Caguas. But the population is recovering under legal protection.
RANGE: Southern North America to northern Chile and Argentina. Typical sites to find this species are at the Boquerón Nature Reserve and the Cabo Rojo salt flats.

Least Bittern
Ixobrychus exilis
Martinetito

A small heron with blackish upperparts contrasting with brown and white underparts. A chestnut or buff-colored wing patch is striking when the bird flies. Length: 28-36 cm.; weight: 80 g. The song is a series of low, rapid cooing notes, much like that of a dove. Lives in shallow marshes or pond edges with tall emergent vegetation; sometimes mangroves. A common, permanent resident; regular at the Humacao Nature Reserve.

Little Blue Heron
Egretta caerulea
Garza Azul

IDENTIFICATION: The adult is slate-blue, with a purplish tinge to the head and neck. The bill is two-colored: gray toward the base, with a dark tip. The immature bird in the first year of life is pure white—like most egret species—but with greenish legs, and a gray bill with a dark tip. Immature birds molting into adult plumage are blotched white and blue (photo below). Length: 56-74 cm.; weight: 352 g.

HABITAT: Fresh and salt water ponds, wetlands, canals, mangrove swamps, estuaries, lagoons, and shallow coastal waters.

HABITS: Usually forages slowly: it walks a short distance through shallow water, then stands still in one place, sometimes twisting its neck slowly for a better view of potential prey. It feeds on crabs, crayfish, insects, other invertebrates, small fish, lizards, and amphibians. Both sexes participate in building a stick nest in a treetop colony near water. In addition to the local breeding population, Little Blue Herons from North America migrate to the Caribbean in winter. Little Blue Herons banded as far away as Mississippi and New Jersey have been recovered in Puerto Rico.

STATUS AND CONSERVATION: Common, permanent resident of Puerto Rico, with the population increasing in winter as migrants arrive. Destruction and pollution of mangrove swamps and other wetlands have decreased habitat for this bird. Because of its dark plumage, this species was not hunted for its feathers, as were other egret and heron species a century ago. However, it was

hunted for food in Puerto Rico.

RANGE: Breeds in the Greater Antilles, the Virgin Islands, Antigua, and the Bahamas; and along both coasts of North America from southern Maine and southern California, south through Central America to Peru and Uruguay. A regular site to find this species is at Parque Central's boardwalk along the Martin Peña canal in San Juan.

Tricolored Heron
Egretta tricolor
Garza Pechiblanca

IDENTIFICATION: Bluish gray with a white belly, and a thin white line up the front of the neck. Length: 66 cm.; weight: 300-400 g.

HABITAT: Forages mostly in shallow, salt water such as mangrove swamps, estuaries, lagoons, and shallow coastal waters.

HABITS: Feeds mostly on small fish, but occasionally eats amphibians and invertebrates. This heron usually forages alone, and has a very active feeding style---chasing fish with its feet and waving its wings like a cowboy herding cattle. It nests in treetop colonies, often with other species of herons. During nest building, the male rarely eats, if at all, while he hunts for twigs, delivers nesting material with much ceremony, and then guards the female while she builds the nest in preparation for the 3-4 blue-green eggs. Both sexes incubate the eggs in alternating 2-6 hour shifts during the 21-25 day incubation period. After several weeks, the young can swim, and can climb by pulling themselves up with their bill, feet and wings. The young begin to fly after 25-30 days, but the parents continue to feed them until 50-56 days after hatching.

STATUS AND CONSERVATION: Common, permanent resident of Puerto Rico, with the population increasing in winter as migrants arrive from North America. Tricolored Herons banded as far away as New Jersey have been recovered in Puerto Rico. Destruction and contamination of mangrove swamps and other marine wetlands have impacted this bird. It is particularly sensitive to human disturbance around nesting colonies. In some parts of its range, aquaculturists illegally shoot this species at fish farms.

RANGE: Breeds in the Greater Antilles, the Bahamas, and some of the eastern Caribbean islands; and along the coast of North America from

southern Maine to northeastern Mexico, and from the Gulf of California to El Salvador. In South America the Tricolored Heron also breeds on both coasts of Colombia, south to the mouth of the Amazon, and on the Pacific coast south to Peru. In Puerto Rico, regular at the Boquerón Nature Reserve and San Juan's Parque Central.

Cattle Egret *Bubulcus ibis*
Garza del Ganado
Garza Ganadera

IDENTIFICATION: A small, white heron with a thick, yellow bill. In breeding season, it develops bright rufous feathers on the head and back. Its wing beat is faster and shallower than that of larger herons and egrets.
Length: 45-56 cm.; weight: 270-512 g.
HABITAT: Typically in pastures, fields, grassy roadsides, municipal landfills. It has also been observed foraging in shallow estuaries, lagoons, tidal pools and along rocky coastlines.
HABITS: Forages alone or in flocks near farm animals, especially cattle and horses, plucking insects stirred up by the large mammals. Besides grasshoppers, crickets, and other insects, it also eats lizards, frogs, crayfish, centipedes, spiders, and the eggs and chicks of other birds when the opportunity arises. Large flocks feed at landfills. It sometimes rides on the back of a cow or horse for short distances, and will flock around farm equipment that flushes insects and other prey from fields. Large flocks roost in trees at night: these roosts can be seen from far away, looking like lit-up Christmas trees. At dawn, small flocks disperse from the roosts to feeding grounds sometimes several kilometers away. In the breeding season the Cattle Egret forms large colonies---often with other heron species---in mangroves or wooded swamps. The male attracts a female to a small treetop breeding territory and ceremoniously brings her twigs for nest building. The female actually constructs the nest, and lays 3-4 light blue eggs. Both sexes share incubation duties for 22-25 days. Both sexes brood and feed the young, and will also shade the chicks during the mid-day heat for the first 10 days. When a parent arrives at the nest, the oldest chick grabs the parent's bill and the parent regurgitates food. Chicks often fight each other, and squabble over food. The two oldest chicks usually win these fights, and on rare occasions, they even kill a younger chick. The older chicks may have an additional advantage besides size: the egg yolks that produce the two older chicks have higher levels of androgen hormones that promote aggressiveness. Chicks fledge at about 30 days of age, and forage on their own at about 60 days. The Cattle Egret starts to breed at about two years of age.
STATUS AND CONSERVATION: Common, permanent resident of Puerto Rico. The Cattle Egret's range expanded dramatically over the last century. It occasionally crosses the southern Atlantic Ocean from Africa to South America. It became an established breeder in northern South America by about 1930. The Cattle Egret then dispersed farther north, possibly in the company of migrating, native herons. It reached Florida by 1942, Puerto Rico by 1948, and Alaska by 1981.
By 1977, the species had been reported from as far south as Tierra del Fuego. One theory is that the Cattle Egret, like other herons, often crossed the Atlantic from Africa, but that only in the last century has it been able to establish itself thanks to the expansion of ranching. This species has flourished thanks to the introduction of livestock to Puerto Rico, and the expansion of open pastureland and agricultural fields. The Cattle Egret benefits farmers by controlling insect pests around livestock.
RANGE: Breeds from southern Canada south to central Argentina and Chile; and in the Old World, through parts of Africa, southern Europe, and southern Asia to Australia.

Green Heron *Butorides virescens*
Martinete

IDENTIFICATION: A small, gray-green heron with a rufous neck. Immatures are duller and more streaked. This species has also been called the Little Green Heron and Green-backed Heron. Length: 41-46 cm.; weight: 240 g.

HABITAT: Fresh and salt water marshes, *Pterocarpus* forest, ponds, canals, mangroves, stream borders, calm ocean shores, wet fields, even gardens.

HABITS: Usually forages alone by crouching on a riverbank or low branch and waiting for prey. It is Puerto Rico's only tool-using bird: it occasionally uses bait (twigs, leaves, worms, flies) to attract small fish within reach. It sometimes plunges into shallow water after prey, and will eat crabs, crayfish, insects, and other invertebrates, as well as fish, frogs, and lizards. Although often hidden in streamside vegetation, this species sometimes perches on wires, branches, or fences, and is often seen flying at treetop level between roosts and feeding areas. Makes a loud "*skeow*" call when disturbed. The Green Heron often nests alone, but sometimes nests in treetop colonies with other heron species. The male breaks off twigs and passes them to the female for nest building. She lays 3-5 blue-green eggs. Both sexes share incubation duties for 19-21 days, and subsequently brood and feed the chicks for the first three weeks after hatching. Chicks can fly about 21-22 days after hatching. Birds nesting in eastern North America winter along the Gulf of Mexico and in the West Indies. One Green Heron banded in Maryland was recovered in Puerto Rico.

STATUS AND CONSERVATION: Common, permanent resident of Puerto Rico, with migrant birds increasing the population in winter. Has benefited from some forms of development, such as golf-course water traps.

RANGE: Breeds from southeastern Canada and British Columbia, south through the Greater Antilles and lowland Central America to Panama and Tobago. Regular in most wetlands.

Yellow-crowned Night-Heron *Nyctanassa violacea* Yaboa Común

IDENTIFICATION: The adult has a gray body, and a striking black-and-white head pattern. Thin white feathers extend behind the crown, but are hard to see from a distance. This night-heron's bill is stouter than in the less common Black-crowned Night-Heron. The immature bird is brown with white spots (smaller than the spots on the immature Black-crowned Night-Heron). Length: 51-70 cm.; weight: 652 g.

HABITAT: Saltwater swamps, lagoons, estuaries, mudflats and ocean shores.

HABITS: Feeds mostly at night on small crabs, although it also eats insects, small fish, and other prey, including eggs and chicks of other bird species. It is the least active feeder among the heron species, and stands still for long periods, waiting for prey. The Yellow-crowned Night-Heron is quite often seen flying at dawn or dusk between feeding grounds and daytime roosts in swamp trees. It sometimes makes a squawking noise as it flies. It nests in small colonies located 8-20 m. high in treetops. The bulky nest is made of sticks and contains 2-5 light blue eggs. Both male and female incubate the eggs for about 21-25 days and both care for the young. Chicks fledge at about 25 days. This species does not breed until two years of age.

STATUS AND CONSERVATION: A common, permanent resident. Many night-herons migrate from eastern North America to winter in the Caribbean. Because it is most active at night, the Yellow-crowned Night-Heron is more common than many people realize. But its breeding habitat has shrunk as wetlands are destroyed. It was formerly hunted in Puerto Rico.

RANGE: Southeastern North America to Brazil. Regular at Cabo Rojo and at Parque Central in San Juan.

Black-crowned Night-Heron
Nycticorax nycticorax
Yaboa Real

This species has a black back, white underparts, and a white head with a black cap. Length: 58-66 cm.; weight: 727-1,014 g. An uncommon and local, permanent resident in marshes in Puerto Rico. Regular in mangroves at the Boquerón Nature Reserve.

44

Reddish Egret
Egretta rufescens
Garza Roja

A medium-sized heron that has two color forms: one is purple with a reddish head and neck, while the other is all white. In both phases, the bill is red with a black tip. The duller immature has a gray bill. Length: 70-80 cm.; weight: 700-850 g. Breeds on the coast of the southern USA, Central America, Cuba, Bahamas and the Cayman Islands. Rare visitor to saltwater wetlands and tidal channels such as at Cabo Rojo.

Glossy Ibis
Plegadis falcinellus
Ibis Lustroso

A dark brown, iridescent wading bird with a long, curved bill. The breeding adult (right photo) has a white line bordering the top and side of the bill. Non-breeding birds have a streaked head. Length: 49-66 cm.; weight: 485-580 g. Breeds in lowlands of the southeastern USA, Cuba, Jamaica, Hispaniola, and in the Old World. Rare breeder and migrant in wetlands such as Laguna Cartagena National Wildlife Refuge and Caño Tiburones Nature Reserve.

White Ibis
Eudocimus albus
Ibis Blanco

A white wading bird with black wing tips, and a long, decurved red bill. Immature birds are brown, but lack the iridescence of the Glossy Ibis. Length: 56-71 cm.; average weight: male 764 g., female 1,036 g. Breeds in lowlands from the southeastern USA to coastal Ecuador, and on Cuba and Hispaniola. Rare visitor and breeder.

Roseate Spoonbill *Platalea ajaja* **Cuchareta**

A long-legged, bright pink bird with a spatula-shaped bill. Length: 71-86 cm.; weight: 1,200-1,800 g. A rare visitor to Puerto Rico, although it is common in nearby Hispaniola. It breeds from southern Texas to northern Argentina, and on Cuba and Hispaniola. It feeds by swinging its bill back and forth in water or mud. Vibration detectors inside its bill sense the presence of food. It has occasionally occurred at the Boquerón Nature Reserve in recent years, most likely dispersing from Hispaniola.

Double-crested Cormorant
Phalacrocorax auritus
Corúa Crestada

A large, dark waterbird with a hooked bill and an orange throat. Length: 70-90 cm.; weight: 1,200-2,500 g. Forages in fresh and salt water ponds and lagoons. The cormorant pursues fish under water, and has legs that are set far back on the body to aid in swimming. It also uses the legs to get a running start across the water to become airborne. Unlike some other diving birds, the cormorant's feathers can get soaked upon entering the water, so the cormorant often spends long periods with its wings extended, drying the feathers in the sun. Does not breed until 3 years of age. In China, Japan, and Europe, people used several species of cormorants to catch fish. They put a ring around the neck to prevent the bird from swallowing the fish. Breeds in North America, Cuba and the Bahamas. In winter, inland breeders move south as far as the Caribbean. Formerly rare, this cormorant has become a regular visitor throughout Puerto Rico and Culebra.

West Indian Whistling-Duck
Dendrocygna arborea
Chiriría

IDENTIFICATION: A mottled brown duck with black and white markings on the sides. In flight, its legs extend beyond its tail. Length: 48-58 cm.; weight: 1,150 g.

HABITAT: Fresh and saltwater wetlands, including lagoons, rice fields, and palm savannas, especially near mangroves, *Pterocarpus*, or other swamp-adapted trees.

HABITS: Feeds at night on fruits, berries, seeds, grass, rice, and corn, and is particularly fond of the fruit of the royal palm (*Roystonea* sp.). It feeds both in trees and on the ground, but less often in open water. It roosts during the day in dense grass or trees such as *Pterocarpus*, where it can be hard to detect with its brown plumage. It nests near water in tree holes, bromeliads, *Panicum* grass, in tree stumps, or in clumps of palm leaves. The nest usually contains 6-12 eggs, and the incubation period is about 30 days.

STATUS AND CONSERVATION: This species is endangered throughout its range. It was once common in Puerto Rico, with flocks of 100 birds reported, but the island population may be only 250. Hunting them is illegal, and some wetland sanctuaries have been expanded to protect its habitat.

RANGE: Endemic to the West Indies. Regular at the Humacao Nature Reserve.

Blue-winged Teal   *Anas discors*   **Pato Zarcel**

A small duck with a brown body and a blue wing patch, especially evident in flight. In breeding plumage the male has a steel-gray head with a white crescent in front. Length: 35-41 cm.; weight: 266-410 g. Breeds in North America. This bird is the most common, migrant duck species that winters in Puerto Rico. Individual Blue-winged Teal that have been banded as far away as Alberta and British Columbia in Canada have been recovered in Puerto Rico---after migrating more than 3,000 miles. 95% of ducks shot by hunters in Puerto Rico each winter are Blue-winged Teal. Worldwide, its population varies with rainfall in the breeding range, but may be as high as 9,000,000 in the fall after a successful breeding season. Spends the winter on fresh and salt water ponds, lagoons and mangrove swamps. Travels in small flocks and feeds on vegetation near the water's surface, or by dipping its head into the water. This feeding behavior is called "dabbling," as opposed to diving---the other major type of duck feeding behavior.

Northern Shoveler   *Anas clypeata*   **Pato Cuchareta**

A dabbling duck with an iridescent green head, white breast and rich brown sides. The female is a mottled brown color. Both sexes have a light blue wing-patch and a flat, broad bill---one of the most unusual bills of any Puerto Rican bird. Length: 45-50 cm.; weight: 400-800 g. A rare, winter visitor. A Northern Shoveler banded in Alberta, Canada, was once recovered in Puerto Rico.

American Wigeon
Anas americana
Pato Cabeciblanco

A small duck with a bluish bill, a brown body, a white cap, and an iridescent, green patch behind the eye. The female has a light gray head, contrasting with a light brown body. The Wigeon has a large white wing patch visible in flight. Length: 45-56 cm.; weight: 680-770 g. It feeds by dabbling: it grazes near the surface or dips its head in shallow water for food. It eats both aquatic plants and invertebrates, and also grazes on grasses on land. An uncommon, migrant duck species wintering in Puerto Rico. Its North American population has been as high as 6,500,000 after a good nesting season in the 1970s, but wetland drainage has put pressure on breeding populations. Banded wigeon from as far away as Prince Edward Island in Canada have been recovered in Puerto Rico.

DOMESTIC DUCKS

Many farmers allow domestic ducks to wander freely, sometimes breeding in the wild.

Mallard
Anas
platyrhynchos
Pato Inglés

A brown duck with an iridescent green head, blue wing patch, white neck ring, and yellow bill. The female and non-breeding male are brown with a mottled bill. Length: 50-65 cm.; weight: 1,000-1,300g. Some may be winter migrants.

Muscovy Duck
Cairina moschata
Pato Real

This duck has fleshy, reddish knobs on its face and bill. Plumage can vary from all white, to glossy black with a white wing patch. The photo above shows two Muscovies mating. Length: 66-84 cm.; weight: 1,100-4,000 g.

Northern Pintail   *Anas acuta*   Pato Pescuecilargo

A dabbling duck with a long neck, and a long, thin tail, obvious in silhouette, even from a distance. The male has a brown head and white neck, while the dull brown female has a shorter, but still pointed tail. Length: males: 57-76 cm.; females: 51-63 cm.; weight: 715-1,000 g. It spends the winter on freshwater marshes and ponds, bays, and flooded fields. The Pintail feeds in the evening and sometimes at night in shallow marshes and flooded fields on seeds, tubers, snails, crustaceans, and insects. It feeds by tipping its upper body into the water, and also occasionally grazes on dry land. When frightened, it takes off vertically from the water's surface, and can wheel and turn quickly in mid-air. Breeds in North America. A Northern Pintail banded in Nova Scotia was once recovered in Puerto Rico. An uncommon, migrant wintering in Puerto Rico. It was probably more common a century ago before the extensive draining of wetlands in the North American prairies. Before the banning of lead shot, 9% of Pintails were found to have lead in their gizzards. An average of 329,000 are shot by hunters in North America each year.

Ring-necked Duck   *Aythya collaris*   Pato del Medio

A small diving duck with distinctive white bands on the bill. The ring on the neck is not easily seen in the field. The male has a dark back, head and breast with a vertical white stripe just behind the breast. The female is brown with a light eye ring. Length: 43 cm.; average weights: males 768 g., females 686 g. Ring-necked Ducks that breed in central and eastern North America tend to winter in the southeastern States and the Caribbean. One bird banded in New York State was recovered in Puerto Rico. An uncommon, winter visitor to Puerto Rico.

Fulvous Whistling-Duck
Dendrocygna bicolor
Chiriría Amarillenta, Chiriría Achocolatada

A light brown duck with white under the base of the tail. Length: 45-53 cm.; weight: 621-755 g. Like other whistling-ducks, this species is mostly nocturnal, but is more often found on the ground than perched in trees. It feeds in swamps, marshes and fields on fruits, bulbs, and seeds, especially rice. This rare species recently expanded its range onto some of the islands of the West Indies including Puerto Rico. Formerly regular at Laguna Cartagena National Wildlife Refuge, before water levels dropped there; rare at Caño Tiburones Nature Reserve.

49

White-cheeked Pintail
Anas bahamensis
Pato Quijada Colorada

IDENTIFICATION: A brown duck with a white "cheek" and throat. The base of the upper bill is bright red. Length: 38-51 cm.; weight: 474-533 g.
HABITAT: Fresh and salt water ponds, lagoons and mangrove swamps.
HABITS: Travels in small flocks and feeds on seeds and leaves of algae and other aquatic plants. It dips its head into the water or occasionally dives for food. It nests on the ground in dense vegetation near water. The female lays 5-12 eggs. Incubation period is about 25 days. Young birds also eat snails, and insects such as water boatmen. White-cheeked Pintail have recently been documented traveling back and forth between Culebra Island and the Humacao marshes in eastern Puerto Rico.
STATUS AND CONSERVATION: Although common elsewhere in the West Indies, the population in Puerto Rico is estimated at only 1,000 birds. Most are found on the eastern end of the island from Yabucoa to Fajardo, as well as on Culebra and Vieques. They are also found in the west, e.g., at Punta Guaniquilla, Cabo Rojo, and the Caño Tiburones and Boquerón nature reserves. Destruction of wetlands, the introduction of the mongoose, and hunting all contributed to the decline of this species. If you find any duck marked with a colored tag or other device, please report the sighting to the Departamento de Recursos Naturales y Ambientales.
RANGE: Breeds in the northern West Indies, and northern South America, and also in northern Argentina and southern Brazil. Regular places to find this bird include the ponds at the Humacao Nature Reserve, and Flamenco Lagoon on Culebra.

Lesser Scaup
Aythya affinis
Pato Pechiblanco

A diving duck with an iridescent purple head and gray body. The female has a brown body, with a white patch at the base of the bill. A white line is evident along the trailing edge of the wing in flight. Length: 38-48 cm.; weight: 800-850 g. Spends the winter on fresh-water ponds and marshes and protected saltwater bays. This bird is an uncommon, localized winter visitor. Lesser Scaup banded as far away as New York State, and Alberta, Canada, have been recovered in Puerto Rico. In the late 1990s, many populations of North American ducks had increased due to favorable, wet weather conditions on the breeding grounds, but populations did not improve for the scaup. On average, 340,000 Lesser Scaup are shot by hunters each year in North America. Breeds from central Alaska east to Quebec, and south through the northern Great Plains and northern Rocky Mountains. It winters from southwestern Canada and the northeastern USA, south through Central America, the Bahamas and Greater Antilles. The Humacao and Caño Tiburones nature reserves are regular locations for this species in winter.

Masked Duck
Nomonyx dominicus
Pato Dominico

IDENTIFICATION: The male has a rufous brown body, black head, and light blue bill. In winter the male molts into a plumage similar to the female's, with two prominent dark horizontal lines on the head, and a gray bill. Length: 30-36 cm.; average weight: males 406 g., females 339 g.

HABITAT: Shallow fresh and brackish water ponds, lagoons, swamps, and flooded fields with plenty of floating or marsh vegetation.
HABITS: Feeds on seeds, roots and shoots of aquatic plants, and some insects and crustaceans. It can dive for its food and uses its tail as a rudder to steer under water. This species stays hidden in dense aquatic vegetation much of the time. When flying off the water, the Masked Duck can take off vertically. This is an adaptation that allows the Masked Duck to safely forage in tiny pools. During the rainy season, the female makes a simple nest of reeds and grasses---with a roof to hide the nest---and lays 3-6 white or buffy eggs. The Masked Duck will also lay its eggs in other waterbirds' nests. The female incubates the eggs for about 28 days. The young leave the nest within two days of hatching, and the male helps the female feed and protect the young.
STATUS AND CONSERVATION: A rare resident in Puerto Rico; the draining of wetlands has reduced potential habitat.
RANGE: Breeds from the Caribbean islands and coastal Mexico south to Colombia, Argentina, and Uruguay. Regular at the Humacao and Caño Tiburones nature reserves.

Ruddy Duck
Oxyura jamaicensis
Pato Chorizo

IDENTIFICATION: A small duck with a rufous brown body, white cheek patches, and a blue bill. The dull female is similar to the rarer Masked Duck, but has one prominent bar below the eye, rather than two. Length: 35-43 cm.; weight: 310-795 g.
HABITAT: Ponds, lagoons, marshes and lakes with emergent vegetation.
HABITS: Travels in small flocks and feeds on aquatic insects, snails, molluscs, worms, and other invertebrates. When danger approaches, the Ruddy Duck dives and emerges a surprising distance away from its starting point. The female builds a nest hidden in marsh vegetation, and lays 6-8 white eggs. Outside the breeding season, this species forms large flocks.

STATUS AND CONSERVATION: An uncommon and threatened nesting species in Puerto Rico, but numbers increase with winter migrants. Population levels have declined due to hunting and drainage of wetlands.
RANGE: Breeds in western Canada and the USA, in the Caribbean, and in western South America. North American breeders migrate to the southern USA, Mexico and the Caribbean for the winter. Regular places to see this species are at the Humacao and Caño Tiburones nature reserves, and Serrallés Lakes near Ponce.

Osprey
Pandion haliaetus
Águila de Mar

IDENTIFICATION: A large hawk: brown above and white below, with a white head and dark eye-stripe. Length: 55-58 cm.; weight: males 1,200-1,600 g., females 1,600-2,000 g.; wingspan: 145-170 cm.

HABITAT: Sea coasts, lakes, salt-flats, mangroves, and along larger rivers, even in urban areas.

HABITS: The Osprey flaps 10-50 m. above the water searching for fish, and then plunges, feet-first into the water to grab its prey. The Osprey's anatomy is so specialized to capture fish that taxonomists classify it in its own subfamily (*Pandioninae*), distinct from other hawks. Its feet have thick scales with spikes on them that prevent fish from slipping off the extremely curved talons. The Osprey typically flies with its fish catch held head-first. In addition to fish, the Osprey occasionally captures crustaceans, birds and rodents.

Frigatebirds will sometimes steal fish from the Osprey. The call is a slow, high-pitched series of whistled notes. Birds found in Puerto Rico in the winter are from populations that breed in North America. Both sexes build a huge stick nest and typically raise 1-2 young in a brood. Incubation is done mostly by the female for 35-43 days. After the eggs hatch, the male brings fish to the female who then feeds the chicks. The young fledge about 50 days after hatching. The Osprey can start breeding at 3 years of age, but 2/3 of the chicks do not survive to breeding age.

STATUS AND CONSERVATION: A winter visitor to Puerto Rico. Its North American breeding population crashed in the mid-20th Century after environmental contamination by the insecticide DDT caused eggshell thinning. With the banning of the pesticide, the Osprey is recovering (breeding populations increased by 6.5% per year between 1966-1995). Sightings have become increasingly common in coastal Puerto Rico in winter. Ospreys have been banded as far away as New York State and later recovered in Puerto Rico.

RANGE: Breeds in temperate latitudes from western Alaska to Florida, as well as in Cuba, Eurasia and coastal Australia. Has attempted to nest on Hispaniola and Puerto Rico. In the New World, it winters from the southern USA through the Caribbean and in coastal South America south to Chile and Argentina. It can be seen over shallow Puerto Rican waters, even along urban coastlines such as Isla Verde.

Turkey Vulture
Cathartes aura
Aura Tiñosa

IDENTIFICATION: A large, black, soaring bird with a red head (gray in the first few months of life). The underside of the flight feathers flash a silvery reflection at the right angle. Length: 64-81 cm.; weight: 850-2,000 g.; wingspan: 180-200 cm.

HABITAT: Open grasslands, coasts, dry forest, pastures and farming country.

HABITS: The Turkey Vulture is often seen soaring over open country as it looks for animal carcasses. To save energy, it glides on the lightest winds, or sometimes soars to great heights in rising hot air. It holds its wings in a "V"-shaped (dihedral) angle that can be distinguished from far away. The vulture often rocks from side to side, as it maneuvers in the breeze. The feathers on the wingtips are often spread apart to reduce air turbulence and decrease the stall speed. Thus the bird can soar very slowly. It detects dead animals by sight or by smell, and will eat any dead animal: mammals, birds, reptiles, amphibians, fish—even dead crickets. As soon as one vulture homes in on a carcass, other vultures seem to appear out of nowhere. The vulture can hop or run short distances, but its feet are weak, so it cannot pull a dead animal very far. This creates a danger when the carcass is a road kill in the middle of a highway. The vulture can survive for weeks between meals. The Turkey Vulture roosts in flocks on exposed tree branches, caves, or cliffs, and can often be seen perched with its wings outspread to dry off and warm up on a cool morning. In the heat of mid-day, vultures can radiate excess heat through the naked skin of the head, and will also urinate on their legs to cool off. The nest is an unmodified rock ledge, cave, tree stump, or just a protected spot under dense shrubs. Vultures are thought to mate for life. Typically two eggs are laid, weighing about 80 g. each. Nest mates alternate incubation duties over a 38-40 day period. The young start to make extended flights 70-80 days after hatching.

STATUS AND CONSERVATION: A common sight in the open country of southcentral and southwestern Puerto Rico. This species was introduced from Cuba in the late 19th Century, presumably to eliminate animal carcasses. Collisions with cars and towers are hazards to the vulture, especially during take off. Pesticide poisoning is a threat, e.g., DDT thinned vulture egg shells before that insecticide was banned. Dogs can attack vultures at roost sites, and mongooses are thought to rob nests.

RANGE: Breeds in the Greater Antilles, and from southern Canada south to Tierra del Fuego, and even the Falkland Islands (Malvinas). During any sunny, mid-day drive from Ponce to Cabo Rojo, at least 50 vultures can usually be seen soaring over open country either in small flocks or alone.

Sharp-shinned Hawk
Accipiter striatus
Halcón de Sierra, Gavilán de Sierra, Falcón de Sierra

IDENTIFICATION: A small forest hawk, dark blue-gray above, barred with rufous on the breast. Immatures are brown above and streaked below (photo at upper left). The wings are broad, and the barred tail is proportionately long. Length: 25-34 cm.; weight: males 95 g., females 171 g.; wingspan 51-69 cm.

HABITAT: In Puerto Rico, currently restricted to five isolated mountain forest areas.

HABITS: Feeds primarily on small birds ranging in size from a tanager down to a hummingbird. Its long tail allows it to turn sharply as it flies after birds in dense vegetation. The adult female is as much as 50% larger than the male, a characteristic called sexual dimorphism. This allows each sex to focus on different-sized prey species. The Puerto Rican subspecies of Sharp-shinned Hawk (*Accipiter striatus venator*) requires a home range of about 150 hectares. When the white eggs are laid in March and April, the female spends most of her time incubating, and relies on the male for food. Average clutch size in one Puerto Rican study was 2.6 eggs, with an incubation period of 32 days. Young fledge and leave the nest about 30 days after hatching.

STATUS AND CONSERVATION: Common in North America, but the smaller, darker subspecies in Puerto Rico is on the federal endangered species list, with a total estimated population of only 154 individuals in 1992. The subspecies experienced a 40% decline in population from 1985 to 1992. Although the regeneration of natural forest since the early 20th Century has helped this bird, recent deforestation due to construction of roads, power lines, and communication facilities, have reduced habitat. In addition, nest failures have been attributed to fledglings infested with bot fly larvae (*Philornis* sp.). Pearly-eyed Thrashers may prey on hawk nests directly, but also rob the nests of small birds and thus may reduce bird populations that the hawk depends on. Sharp-shinned Hawks will occasionally kill young chickens, and as a result, farmers have persecuted the hawks. However, all birds of prey are protected by Commonwealth and federal law.

RANGE: Breeds in North America, Cuba, Hispaniola and Puerto Rico. The endemic subspecies in Puerto Rico is now found only in five public forest areas: Maricao, Toro Negro, Guilarte and Carite State Forests, and Caribbean National Forest (El Yunque).

Broad-winged Hawk
Buteo platypterus
Guaraguao de Bosque

IDENTIFICATION: A medium-sized forest hawk; it is brown above, and light rufous below, with light wing linings visible in flight. The tail is boldly barred with broad, black and white bands. Length: 34-44 cm.; weight: 265-550 g.; wingspan 86-100 cm. The female is slightly larger than the male. The Puerto Rican subspecies (*Buteo platypterus brunnescens*) falls in the smaller size range for the species.

HABITAT: Currently found only in a few isolated mountain areas in both natural and plantation forests.

HABITS: Prefers to hunt from a perch under the forest canopy that offers a clear view of a forest clearing, trail, river, or road. It also flies just above the forest canopy hunting for frogs, lizards, birds,

large insects, and centipedes. Each pair requires a home range of about 40 hectares. The Broad-winged Hawk typically builds its stick nest in February and March and lays 2-4 white eggs with brown splotches. The female incubates the eggs for 28-31 days, while the male hunts for food. After hatching, the larger chick in a clutch may try to kill the smaller chicks. The young fledge in April and May about 29-31 days after hatching, and can fly well about six weeks after hatching. The parents feed the young birds for the first few weeks after leaving the nest.

STATUS AND CONSERVATION: Common in North America, but the subspecies in Puerto Rico is on the federal endangered species list, with a total estimated population of only 124 individuals in 1992. This bird was common in the mid-19th Century, but had become so rare that some biologists thought it extinct in Puerto Rico by the early 20th Century. In the Caribbean National Forest, Broad-winged Hawks declined by 50% from 1984 to 1992. Illegal hunting and forest destruction due to construction of roads, power lines, and communication facilities are threats to this species. Due to the small, isolated populations of this species, major hurricanes are a potential threat. Protection of nest sites and coordination of forest management to protect and enhance the hawks' forest habitat is essential.

RANGE: Breeds in North America, and the West Indies where four subspecies occur on other islands. North American populations migrate for the winter to southern Florida and Guatemala south to southern Peru and Brazil. The endemic subspecies in Puerto Rico is essentially found only in three forest areas: Río Abajo and Carite State Forests; and Caribbean National Forest (El Yunque). The highest density in recent surveys has been in the Río Abajo State Forest. Although it can be seen soaring, the hawk's preference for hunting from a perch or gliding low over the forest canopy make it difficult to detect.

Red-tailed Hawk   *Buteo jamaicensis*   Guaraguao

IDENTIFICATION: A large, brown hawk with rounded wings. Although it does have a reddish tail, that color is not easily seen from below. The dark belly band on the light undersides is a more reliable field mark. Some individuals are much darker below, while juveniles have streaked undersides. The Spanish conquerors adopted a Native American name for this species. Length: 56 cm.; weight: males 690-1,300 g.; females 900-1,460 g.; wingspan 127 cm.

HABITAT: Forested areas and forest edges, even over cities.

HABITS: The Red-tailed Hawk often sits on a perch to watch for prey below, and then glides down to catch rodents, crabs, lizards, small birds, large insects (crickets, grasshoppers), even large centipedes. It will also fly above the forest canopy or suburban landscapes looking for prey. Smaller birds sometimes chase the Red-tailed Hawk out of their territory. In fact, a popular expression in Puerto Rico is "cada guaraguao tiene su pitirre" which means, "every hawk has its kingbird" [pestering it]. The Red-tail has a dramatic courtship flight, with the male and female calling, circling each other, and soaring high in the air. The call is a descending *"keeer"*, like steam escaping from a boiler. Its nest is a large jumble of sticks in the crown of a tree and contains 2-3 white eggs. Both sexes build the

nest, incubate the eggs and feed the chicks. The incubation period is 28-35 days, and the chicks leave the nest 42-46 days after hatching. But the young birds stay close to their parents for several months after fledging. Captive Red-tailed Hawks have lived as long as 29 years.

STATUS AND CONSERVATION: A common sight over forests and forest edges, even in urban areas. The Red-tailed Hawk was formerly hunted extensively, in part because it makes an easy target when gliding, and also because farmers were concerned about the occasional chicken it might capture. Hawk nestlings were reportedly taken for food by farmers in Puerto Rico a century ago. Under legal protection, the population may well be higher now than early in the 20th Century.

RANGE: Breeds from central Alaska south through the Caribbean to Panama. A regular site for this species is over the forests of El Yunque.

American Kestrel   *Falco sparverius*   **Halcón Común**

IDENTIFICATION: A small falcon with distinct plumages in males and females. Both sexes have a reddish tail and prominent black lines below and behind the eye. The male has blue wings, spotted undersides, and black "eye spots" on the back of the neck; while the female has reddish brown wings and streaked undersides. Even from a distance, a perched kestrel can often be identified by its habit of dramatically bobbing its long tail up and down. Length: 23-30 cm.; weight: males 80-143 g., females 84-165 g.; wingspan 51-61 cm.

HABITAT: Farms, pastures, and open country; towns with gardens and trees, especially on the drier, southern side of the island.

HABITS: The Kestrel is often seen on an exposed perch (tree branch, palm frond, or telephone pole) as it searches for food. It will drop from the perch to catch a lizard or large insect, such as a grasshopper or cricket, but will also hover over one place looking for prey, and then attack from the air. Whereas insects and lizards are common prey, it less commonly feeds on birds, mice, or bats. It sometimes stores food for later meals. Kestrels in Europe have been documented to track rodents by detecting their urine and feces in ultraviolet light. It is not known if kestrels in Puerto Rico use the same strategy. Kestrels can be aggressive and will chase Red-tailed Hawks from their territory. The call is a string of *"killy"* notes. The nest is an unimproved ledge, tree hole or simply a flat spot in the top of a royal palm. Both sexes incubate 2-4 eggs for 27-32 days and then feed the young until they fledge at 29-31 days.

STATUS AND CONSERVATION: A common, nesting species especially in open country; probably became more common with forest clearing over the last few centuries.

RANGE: Breeds from Alaska to Tierra del Fuego in Argentina. Most individuals from Canada and the northern USA migrate south in winter, and some travel to the Caribbean.

Merlin
Falco columbarius
Halcón Migratorio

IDENTIFICATION: A small falcon, with heavy streaking below, and contrasting dark and light bars on the tail. The male has a blue-gray back, while the larger female has a brown back. Length: 24-33 cm.; weight: males 165 g., females 230 g.

HABITAT: In winter, the Merlin occurs at edges of agricultural areas, coasts, saltflats, clearings in wet, dry and elfin forest, and in towns.

HABITS: Over 90% of its diet consists of small birds, up to the size of sandpipers. It surprises its prey from an open perch or by flying low over open areas

STATUS AND CONSERVATION: Uncommon winter resident in Puerto Rico. Most Merlins that breed in northeastern North America winter in the Caribbean. Merlins banded in New York State and Wisconsin have been recovered in Puerto Rico. This species suffered from eggshell thinning during the mid-20th Century due to exposure to DDT and other persistent pesticides. It still suffers from illegal shooting, collisions with cars and towers, and destruction of breeding and wintering habitat. The Merlin is popular in the sport of falconry.

RANGE: Breeds in northern North America. A regular location to find it is near mudflats at Cabo Rojo, where it patrols the shores looking for sandpipers.

Peregrine Falcon
Falco peregrinus
Halcón Peregrino

IDENTIFICATION: A medium-sized hawk with dark gray upperparts and a wedge-shaped patch below the eye that gives the falcon a helmeted look. In flight, this falcon has long, pointed wings. Length: 36-58 cm.; weight: 530-1,500 g.

HABITAT: In winter, prefers edges of agricultural areas, marshes, wetlands, saltflats, and rocky islands; occasionally taller city buildings near parks frequented by Rock Pigeons.

HABITS: The Peregrine has been the prized hunting bird of falconers since the Middle Ages. It feeds on some small mammals and lizards, but mostly on birds, such as sandpipers, ducks, and city pigeons.

STATUS AND CONSERVATION: An uncommon winter visitor to Puerto Rico, the Peregrine Falcon had been on the federal endangered species list. After World War II, the use of the insecticide DDT, and other organochlorine chemicals, such as PCBs, caused Peregrines to lay thin-shelled eggs that broke during incubation. By 1975, the population reached a low of 324 nesting pairs in North America. Recovery efforts include a ban on the use of DDT, the protection of nest sites, captive breeding programs, and reintroduction efforts. As a result of this recovery effort, at least 1,640 pairs bred in North America in 1999, and it has been removed from the endangered species list. Peregrine sightings have become more common in Puerto Rico including on the Cabo Rojo Chistmas Bird Count.

RANGE: One of the most widespread bird species in the world. It once bred throughout much of North America, and south in the Andes to Tierra del Fuego. In winter, northern Peregrine populations migrate widely (hence the name, "peregrine"), as far south as northeastern South America.

Purple Gallinule
Porphyrio martinica
Gallareta Inglesa
Gallareta Azul

IDENTIFICATION: The Purple Gallinule has a bright purple body, greenish back, and a red and yellow bill. Length 32-35 cm.; weight: 310-456 g.

HABITAT: Freshwater marshes and ponds with dense vegetation.

HABITS: Feeds on plant leaves, seeds and flowers; insects, worms, frogs, and sometimes eggs and chicks of other birds. It walks supported by its long toes on floating vegetation. Calls include reedy, clucking notes. The nest is a bulky mass of plant fragments, sometimes with an entrance ramp. Both sexes incubate the 3-12 eggs for 18-25 days. The parents feed the chicks at the nest for the first 2-4 days, and then the chicks leave the nest except for brooding. Parents continue to feed the chicks until they are three weeks old. Non-breeding birds sometimes help the parents care for the young. Chicks fledge at 5-7 weeks.

STATUS AND CONSERVATION: An uncommon, permanent resident in marshes in Puerto Rico. The drainage of wetlands has decreased habitat for this species.

RANGE: Breeds from southeastern North America, south through the Greater Antilles and some islands of the eastern Caribbean to northern Argentina. The Spanish name of "Gallareta Inglesa" refers to the colors of the bird, not its range. Regular at the Humacao and Caño Tiburones nature reserves.

Common Moorhen
Gallinula chloropus
Gallareta Común

IDENTIFICATION: The Common Moorhen has a blue and gray body with a white line on the side, and a bright red facial shield. Length: 32-35 cm.; weight: 310-456 g.

HABITAT: Freshwater and brackish marshes, canals, ditches, mangroves, and ponds with dense vegetation; also stream banks and lawns.

HABITS: Feeds mostly on algae, plant leaves, and seeds; and less commonly on insects, worms, frogs, and sometimes eggs and chicks of other birds. It forages by dipping its head in the water, or walking on floating vegetation, inspecting under leaves for food. The voice is a stuttering, trumpet-like call note, as well as various clucking noises. Both sexes build the nest on floating vegetation, in a shrub, or on the ground near water. Both sexes incubate the 3-12 eggs for 19-22 days. The female sometimes lays her eggs in other Moorhen's nests. Birds from previous broods help the parents care for the young. Chicks fledge at 6-7 weeks.

STATUS AND CONSERVATION: A common, permanent resident in marshes in Puerto Rico. The ever-increasing number of golf courses with their accompanying water traps could provide potential new habitat for this species.

RANGE: Breeds from eastern North America and California, south to northern Argentina. Regular at the Humacao and Caño Tiburones nature reserves.

59

American Coot
Fulica americana
Gallinazo Americano

IDENTIFICATION: A dark gray waterbird with a red knob above a white bill; it has a smaller, white facial shield than the Caribbean Coot. Length: 34-43 cm.; weight: males 742 g.; females 560 g.

HABITAT: Freshwater lakes, ponds, marshes.

HABITS: Feeds on aquatic plants, plus fish, snails, worms, crustaceans, and insects. It sometimes eats eggs of other birds. It feeds at the water's surface or by diving. Calls include a prolonged, reedy croak. In North America, both sexes build the nest which is a floating platform anchored in marsh vegetation. Both sexes take turns incubating the 8-12 eggs over 21-25 days. Soon after hatching, the chicks leave the nest and follow parents to feed. Chicks fledge at 49-56 days.

STATUS AND CONSERVATION: A common winter visitor from North America ; rarely breeds in Puerto Rico. Coots banded in Delaware and Wisconsin have been recovered in Puerto Rico. The pioneering ornithologist, Alexander Wetmore, said that this species was a common breeder in Puerto Rico in the early 20th Century and that "country people searched the marshes systematically for their eggs, so that few escaped." He noted a flock of 300-400 birds, many of them young, at Laguna Tortuguero Nature Reserve. His informants may have confused the two coot species, or the American Coot bred more commonly in Puerto Rico then.

RANGE: Breeds from southern Canada to Central America and the western Antilles. Winters in the West Indies and southern North

Caribbean Coot   *Fulica caribaea*   **Gallinazo Nativo**

IDENTIFICATION: A dark gray water bird with a large white or yellowish facial shield. The shield is broader at the top than in the American Coot. Length: 33-38 cm. Coots have partially webbed toes that aid in swimming. Taxonomists sometimes lump this species with the American Coot.

HABITAT: Freshwater ponds and marshes.

HABITS: Feeds on algae and other plant leaves and seeds; also insects.

STATUS AND CONSERVATION: An uncommon permanent resident in Puerto Rico. Has declined due to hunting, drainage of wetlands and nest predation by rats, cats, and mongooses.

RANGE: Breeds in the Greater Antilles and Venezuela. Regular at Serrallés Lakes near Ponce and at Caño Tiburones Nature Reserve.

Clapper Rail
Rallus longirostris
Pollo de Mangle

IDENTIFICATION: A shy, chicken-sized marsh bird, grayish-brown above and cinnamon-colored below, with a long, narrow bill. Its body is laterally compressed to allow it to squeeze between vegetation. Length: 32-41 cm.; weight: 160-400 g.
HABITAT: Mangroves and saltwater mudflats.
HABITS: The Clapper Rail is more often heard than seen. It walks on mangrove roots and mudflats, occasionally flicking its tiny tail. It plucks fiddler crabs and other crab species from the surface of mudflats and plants, and will also eat snails, worms, small fish and aquatic insects. It sometimes rinses off its food before swallowing it. The Clapper Rail makes a variety of grunts, "clapping" noises and other calls.
STATUS AND CONSERVATION: A common marsh species, but has probably declined as mangrove swamps have been destroyed. Was heavily hunted for its tasty flesh. A local expression is to call someone "Pollo de Mangle," a joking way of saying that someone is ugly.
RANGE: Breeds from coastal New England and California south to Peru and Brazil, and in much of the West Indies, east to Guadeloupe. Large mangrove stands such as at Cabo Rojo and Boquerón Nature Reserve are regular sites in Puerto Rico.

Sora
Porzana carolina
Gallito

A brown-backed marsh bird with a black face and yellow bill. Length: 20-25 cm.; weight: 72-88 g. A shy, uncommon winter visitor which breeds in freshwater marshes in southern Canada and the northern USA. The Sora eats seeds, insects and snails. Like other rails, it prefers to run from danger rather than fly. It winters from the southern USA south through the West Indies to central South America. In Puerto Rico it inhabits marshes and wet cane fields, and is regular at Caño Tiburones Nature Reserve.

Yellow-breasted Crake
Porzana flaviveter
Gallito Amarillo

A tiny, sparrow-sized marsh bird, with a brown back, yellow breast and black bars on the sides. Length: 12.4-14 cm.; weight: 20-28 g. Inhabits freshwater marshes, pond edges, flooded fields, and ditches with dense vegetation. It tunnels like a mouse through marsh vegetation. Occasionally at dawn or dusk, one will run across a dike, or fly from the edge of a pond or marsh, with its legs dangling below it. However, it is more often heard than seen. It feeds on insects, seeds and crustaceans plucked from water or vegetation. The female lays 3-5 eggs in a nest built in floating vegetation or reeds. An uncommon, permanent resident in Puerto Rico. Wetlands drainage has decreased its habitat. Breeds in the Greater Antilles, and from Mexico to northern Argentina. Recently reported from the Humacao, Caño Tiburones and Boquerón nature reserves and Laguna Cartagena National Wildlife Refuge.

Black-bellied Plover
Pluvialis squatarola
Playero Cabezón

IDENTIFICATION: Plovers have a relatively short bill and short neck, which give them a distinct profile compared to other shorebirds. The Black-bellied Plover is a large shorebird with a light belly, and a gray-brown back, speckled with white in winter plumage (see upper photo). It has a large-headed and big-eyed look. Before migrating north, the Black-bellied Plover molts into a breeding plumage with black undersides. In flight, the feathers at the base of the underwings (axillars) are black. Length: 28-29 cm.; weight: 180 g.

HABITAT: Mudflats, edges of mangroves, salt flats, and tidal pools on sandy beaches.

HABITS: Feeds alone or in loose association with other shorebird species who benefit from the plover's habit of quickly sounding the alarm at approaching danger. It feeds on a wide variety of marine worms, insects and small molluscs. Its large eyes are presumed to be an adaptation to feeding at night. Plovers typically run instead of walk, and sometimes will swim short distances across small pools. At high tide, small flocks roost on pilings, dikes, in mangroves, on rocks, or on protected higher beaches. Most winter visitors arrive in August or September and leave by late April, but some birds---presumably one-year old birds that have never bred---spend the summer. On the winter grounds, it gives a slurred whistle, and sometimes a three-note contact call *"Pee-o-wee."* During the migration north, birds defend small feeding areas from other plovers. On the breeding range in North America, this species prefers high, dry tundra for nesting. The male digs a small scrape nest on a ridge top that gives it a commanding view for quick detection of predators. When the female accepts a nest site, she adds a lining of lichens and grasses. Each of the four eggs is about 16% of the female's body weight. Both sexes have two large incubation patches (featherless areas of skin on the belly that facilitate transfer of heat). Chicks hatch after 24-27 days of incubation and leave the nest about two days after hatching. The parents brood the young even after they have abandoned the nest, and will lead the chicks to food. The chicks fledge after about 35-45 days. As with many other shorebirds, juvenile birds migrate south after adults have already departed. This species often does not breed until two or three years old.

STATUS AND CONSERVATION: A common species on salt flats and other beaches and mudflats. Because it is so wary of humans, it was not as seriously impacted as other shorebird species by market hunting in the 19th Century.

RANGE: Found over a wide area of coastal habitat in the Old World, where it is called the Grey Plover. In the Western Hemisphere, it nests along the Bering Sea and on the high Arctic islands and coasts of Alaska and Canada. In winter it is restricted to coastal areas from Washington State and Connecticut south along the coasts of Central America and the Caribbean Islands to central Chile and Argentina. Regular at the Cabo Rojo salt flats.

Wilson's Plover
Charadrius wilsonia
Playero Marítimo

IDENTIFICATION: A brown-backed shorebird with a single, broad breast band and a relatively thick bill. Length: 16.5-20 cm.; weight: 55-70 g.

HABITAT: Mudflats and salt pans.

HABITS: The Wilson's Plover is especially fond of crustaceans such as fiddler crabs, and will also eat worms, snails, and insects. It forages relatively slowly, either alone or in flocks of other shorebirds. The call is a high-pitched, pipping note. The male builds several sandy, scrape nests, and tries to attract a female with a courtship dance in which he spreads his wings low and dances around her. Both sexes share in incubating the three eggs for 24-25 days, the female doing most of the incubation in the daytime. Young leave the nest soon after hatching, and fledge after 3-4 weeks.

STATUS AND CONSERVATION: A common, permanent resident. Its ground nest is easily disturbed by humans or predators.

RANGE: Breeds along the southern coasts of North America south to northern Brazil and Colombia. Regular at the Cabo Rojo salt flats and Caño Tiburones Nature Reserve.

Snowy Plover   *Charadrius alexandrinus*   Playero Blanco

IDENTIFICATION: A small shorebird with very pale, sandy-brown upperparts, white underparts, dark bill and legs, and small patches of black on the side of the neck, on the forehead and behind the eye. Length: 15-17 cm.; weight: 34-58 g.

HABITAT: Primarily edges of salt ponds, but potentially on wide, sandy beach areas.

HABITS: Plucks prey off the surface of water, sand and mud, or probes for insect larvae and other invertebrates. It sometimes taps its feet on the surface to scare up prey, and also will snatch flying insects from the air. Pairs form by January. The male starts building a nest depression in

a dry sandy area. During the 25-28 day incubation period, both sexes line the nest with small pebbles and shells. Three eggs are typical in a clutch. Chicks first fly about 28-33 days after hatching.

STATUS AND CONSERVATION: An uncommon, localized permanent resident in Puerto Rico. The nests are vulnerable to predators and human disturbance, so strict protection of breeding areas is essential.

RANGE: Breeds on Hispaniola, Puerto Rico and some of the Bahamas and Virgin Islands; also breeds in North America and the Old World. In Puerto Rico, regularly found at the Cabo Rojo salt flats.

Killdeer
Charadrius vociferus
Playero Sabanero

IDENTIFICATION: A brown-backed shorebird with two black bands across the white breast. Length: 20-28 cm.; weight: 72-93 g.
HABITAT: Pond edges, mudflats, fields of low grass, golf courses, and residential lawns.
HABITS: Forages alone or in small, loose flocks and picks insects and other invertebrates from the surface

of vegetation or mud. It often runs a short distance, then stands still for a minute or two before running to another vantage point. The voice is a loud, high-pitched, *"kill"* or *"kill-deer"*, given when alarmed. The Latin name *vociferus* is very appropriate, since this species sounds a loud alarm at the slightest hint of danger. The male builds a well-camouflaged scrape nest in an exposed gravel area with a commanding view of the surroundings, often returning to the same area for later nestings. Nowadays, the Killdeer often nests on the flat, gravel roofs of buildings in shopping malls and factories where it is safe from ground predators. Both sexes incubate 3-4 eggs for 24-28 days. Since the nests are in vulnerable areas, they often fail, but the Killdeer will try again if the first nest fails. If a predator approaches the nest too closely, one parent will attempt to lure the predator away by flashing its orange rump and pretending that its wing is broken. The chicks leave the nest right after hatching and are protected by the parents for several weeks after they fledge at about four weeks.
STATUS AND CONSERVATION: A common, permanent resident in Puerto Rico. Migrant Killdeer from North America visit Puerto Rico in the winter as well. Clearing of forests for farmland in the 19th Century created habitat for this species, as has the recent boom in golf courses.
RANGE: Breeds from southern Alaska to southern Mexico, along the west coast of South America, and in the Greater Antilles and Bahamas. A regular sight on golf courses and flying over shopping malls especially at dawn and dusk.

Semipalmated Plover
Charadrius semipalmatus
Playero Acollarado

IDENTIFICATION: A small shorebird with a short bill, and black breast and head patches. Duller brown in winter (photo at left). Length: 17-19 cm.; weight: 47 g.
HABITAT: Salt flats, marshes and beaches.
HABITS: Winters in flocks with other shorebirds. Roosts on pilings and higher beaches.

STATUS AND CONSERVATION: A common winter visitor to Puerto Rico. Populations have increased since the end of market hunting of the 19th Century.
RANGE: Breeds in Alaska and northern Canada. Regular at Cabo Rojo.

Black-necked Stilt   *Himantopus mexicanus*   **Viuda**

IDENTIFICATION: A tall shorebird with dramatic black-and-white plumage, and long, pink legs. Length: 35-39 cm.; weight: 136-220 g.

HABITAT: Shallow marshes, swamps, salt ponds, and mangroves.

HABITS: The Stilt travels in noisy flocks, and wades into muddy waters to feed on crustaceans, worms, snails, small fish, and insects such as flies and water boatmen. Its call is a loud, high pitched, "*kek kek kek*", given when alarmed. Other shorebirds rely on it to sound the alarm when humans or predators approach too closely. Both sexes build a scrape nest in grass or on a high area of mudflats, often near other Stilts' nests. Both sexes incubate the 3-6 eggs for 22-26 days. The chicks follow the parents away from the nest soon after hatching and feed themselves. They fledge at 4-5 weeks after hatching, but the parents continue to help them forage for several weeks after that. Stilts start to breed at age 1-2 years.

STATUS AND CONSERVATION: A common, permanent resident in Puerto Rico. Drainage of wetlands has reduced habitat for this species. Formerly hunted, the Stilt is now protected.

RANGE: Breeds from the East Coast and interior West of the USA, south to northern Argentina. Regular in shallow, saltwater pools at Boquerón Nature Reserve and Cabo Rojo. A closely related species is found in Africa, Eurasia, and Australia.

Greater Yellowlegs
Tringa melanoleuca
Playero Guineílla Mayor

IDENTIFICATION: A long-legged shorebird, gray above with a white tail with barring toward the tip. It has dramatic, yellow legs, and a somewhat longer, thicker, and upturned bill when compared to the smaller Lesser Yellowlegs. Length: 29-33 cm.; weight: 111-235 g.
HABITAT: Fresh and saltwater wetlands, pools and mudflats.
HABITS: Feeds on small invertebrates, fish and frogs, occasionally at night. In addition to plucking food from near the water's surface, it may sweep its bill in the water from side to side to detect prey by touch.
STATUS AND CONSERVATION: A common migrant, especially in the fall. It was hunted extensively in the 19ᵗʰ Century, and has become more common since then.
RANGE: Nests in the swampy, boreal forests south of the tundra in southern Canada and southern Alaska---farther south than the Lesser Yellowlegs. It winters along the coast of North America from California and New England south, through the West Indies and Central America to Tierra del Fuego.

Lesser Yellowlegs   *Tringa flavipes*   Playero Guineílla Menor

IDENTIFICATION: A gray-backed shorebird, with long yellow legs. Its bill is shorter, straighter, and thinner than in the larger Greater Yellowlegs. Length: 23-25 cm.; weight: 67-94 g.
HABITAT: Marshes, mudflats, and edges of ponds.
HABITS: Plucks prey off the surface of mudflats and will wade into shallow water to look for food on the surface. Eats insects, worms, snails, small fish, and crustaceans. It flocks with other shorebird species, but sometimes defends choice feeding areas from other yellowlegs. It rocks its body when alarmed. The call is a repeated series of single or double notes, sometimes more. Usually the number of notes is fewer and the call is softer than the call of the Greater Yellowlegs.

STATUS AND CONSERVATION: A common winter resident in Puerto Rico, usually more common than the Greater Yellowlegs.
RANGE: Breeds in Alaska and Canada. A regular place to find both yellowlegs species is the Cabo Rojo salt flats.

Spotted Sandpiper *Actitis macularius* **Playero Coleador**

IDENTIFICATION: This shorebird has an olive-brown back, a white eye line, and white underparts with round spots. The bill is reddish orange with a black tip. In winter, the spots are lacking and the bill duller (right photo). Length: 18-20 cm.; weight: females 43-50 g., males 34-41 g.

HABITAT: Rocky shores, mangroves, mudflats, lake shores, and river banks.

HABITS: The Spotted Sandpiper can be recognized from far away by its unique habit of bobbing its body up and down as it walks---or even when standing in one place. It flies with shallow, quick bursts of its wings, which it points stiffly downward between wing beats. The Spotted Sandpiper is one of only 0.2% of all bird species with a reversal of sex roles. The female is larger and more aggressive in courting the male and will sometimes have 2-4 mates (polyandry) on its breeding grounds in North America. Each male defends its own nesting territory within the female's larger territory.

STATUS AND CONSERVATION: A common winter visitor.

RANGE: Breeds from the edge of the tundra south to the central USA. It winters from the southern USA, through the Caribbean, to northern Chile and central Argentina.

Solitary Sandpiper
Tringa solitaria
Playero Solitario

IDENTIFICATION: A thin sandpiper that bobs its tail as it walks. It has an olive back with white spots, and a white eye ring. Length: 19-23 cm.; weight: 38-69 g.

HABITAT: Small pools of freshwater, ditches, puddles in wetlands, fields and pastures.

HABITS: The Solitary Sandpiper is well named, since it tends to forage and migrate alone or in very small flocks. It plucks insects, spiders, worms and other invertebrates from mud or near the water's surface. It sometimes agitates mud or water with one foot to scare up prey, but will also stay motionless for long periods. As the Solitary Sandpiper lands, it holds its wings up and then slowly folds them. The call, given in flight, consists of three notes---higher in pitch than the call of the commoner Spotted Sandpiper. On the breeding grounds just south of the North American tundra, it is unique among shorebirds: it nests in trees. It finds an abandoned nest of a robin, jay, or other songbird near a pond, and modifies it for its own use. The female lays a clutch of four eggs. Incubation is thought to last 23-24 days, but many details of its breeding biology are unknown.

STATUS AND CONSERVATION: A common fall and spring migrant; rare in winter.

RANGE: Breeds from central Alaska to New Brunswick. It winters from southern Texas and Mexico south through the Greater Antilles to Peru and central Argentina.

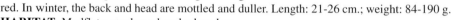

Ruddy Turnstone
Arenaria interpres
Playero Turco

IDENTIFICATION: In breeding plumage has a rufous and black back, and a dramatic, white-and-black head and breast pattern; the short legs are bright red. In winter, the back and head are mottled and duller. Length: 21-26 cm.; weight: 84-190 g.

HABITAT: Mudflats; sandy and rocky beaches.

HABITS: Flips over pebbles and stranded beach algae looking for food. It probes in mud as well, searching for crustaceans, molluscs, insects and worms. On its Arctic breeding grounds, the female builds a simple nest of leaves, twigs and moss on the tundra. Both sexes incubate the 3-4 eggs for 22-24 days. Both parents lead the young away from the nest after hatching, and the chicks immediately feed themselves. Shortly afterward the female abandons them, leaving the male to protect the young until they can fly about 19-21 days after hatching.

STATUS AND CONSERVATION: A common winter resident of Puerto Rico.

RANGE: Breeds on the far northern tundra near the Arctic Ocean in North America and Eurasia. In the Americas, winters from coastal southern USA through South America.

Whimbrel   *Numenius phaeopus*   **Playero Picocorvo**

IDENTIFICATION: A large shorebird with a long, downward-curved bill. It has several dark brown stripes on the head. Length: 35 cm.; weight: 310-493 g.

HABITAT: Shallow saltponds and tidal mudflats.

HABITS: Uses its long, curved bill to extract crabs from curved burrows. It also feeds on marine worms, molluscs, and fish. In North America, the Whimbrel nests in tundra and moist northern forests. The male sets up a territory soon after the snow melts, attracts a female and establishes a monogamous pair bond. The Whimbrel builds a nest in a grassy hummock. Both sexes incubate the 3-4 eggs for 22-28 days. The nest mate that is not incubating stands guard nearby against predators. The young leave the nest shortly after hatching to feed on insects and berries. After a few days, the female abandons the chicks to the care of the male. The young can fly after 30-42 days. In the fall, the Whimbrel migrates to eastern Canada and New England to spend several weeks fattening up on berries and insects before taking off on an open-ocean crossing to the Caribbean and South America. Does not breed until three years of age, but may live to 19 years.

STATUS AND CONSERVATION: A rare, but conspicuous, localized migrant in Puerto Rico. Its North American population is now 25,000-100,000, presumably an increase after the slaughter by market hunters a century ago.

RANGE: Nests in Alaska, northwestern Canada and northern Eurasia. The salt flats at Cabo Rojo are a regular location in winter and migration.

Sanderling
Calidris alba
Playero Arenero

A small shorebird, sandy gray above, and white below. It is browner above in breeding plumage. Length: 18-20 cm.; weight: 40-100 g. The Sanderling typically feeds by following retreating waves, to pluck small molluscs and crustaceans. The Sanderling breeds on the tundra in the high Arctic of North America, Greenland and Siberia. It is an uncommon winter resident in Puerto Rico, usually found in small flocks.

Semipalmated Sandpiper
Calidris pusilla
Playerito Gracioso

IDENTIFICATION: A small, black-legged shorebird, similar to the Western Sandpiper, but without the rufous back feathers in breeding plumage. The bill tends to be shorter and straighter than the Western's. Length: 13-15 cm.; weight: 21-32 g.
HABITAT: Forages on exposed tidal flats, farm ponds, and shallow lagoons in winter and on migration.
HABITS: The Semipalmated Sandpiper forms flocks to feed on insect larvae, worms and molluscs in salt and fresh-water pools. In the fall 75-94% of the world's population of Semipalmated Sandpipers stages at Canada's Bay of Fundy to put on extra fat before migrating thousands of kilometers over open ocean to the West Indies and South America.
STATUS AND CONSERVATION: A common winter visitor. Its population declined during the market hunting days.
RANGE: Breeds on the Arctic tundra. It winters primarily in Surinam and French Guiana. A regular location to find this species is the mudflats near Cabo Rojo.

Western Sandpiper
Calidris mauri
Playerito Occidental

IDENTIFICATION: A small shorebird with dark legs, and a proportionately longer bill than other small sandpipers. The bill sometimes has a drooped tip. In breeding plumage, has rusty flecks on its back. Length:14-17 cm.; weight: 22-36 g.
HABITAT: Forages on exposed tidal marshes and salt flats in migration.

HABITS: The Western Sandpiper travels in flocks, busily following the tide in search of invertebrates.
STATUS AND CONSERVATION: Common winter visitor.
RANGE: Breeds on tundra along the Arctic and Bering Sea coasts. Regular in tidal inlets at Cabo Rojo.

Least Sandpiper
Calidris minutilla
Playerito Menudo
This is the smallest sandpiper in the world. It is a richer brown above than other small shorebirds in the West Indies, and has yellow or greenish-yellow legs. Length: 13-15 cm.; weight: 19-30 g. On migration it prefers grassy marshes, mud-flats, edges of ditches, and flooded pastures and fields. The Least Sandpiper forages in flocks with other species, often favoring the higher, vegetated edges of mudflats. It pecks or probes the surface of mud for insect larvae, crustaceans and other invertebrates. Breeds on tundra and wet forest edges over most of Alaska and northern Canada east to Nova Scotia. Winters in the southern USA, south through Central America and the West Indies to southern Peru and central Brazil.

Pectoral Sandpiper   *Calidris melanotos*   Playero Manchado

IDENTIFICATION: A yellow-legged, medium-sized shorebird with a sharp boundary between the dark breast and light belly. Length: 19 cm.; weight: males 81 g., females 71 g.
HABITAT: Feeds along edges of freshwater wetlands, on mats of algae, and in moist, dense grasslands.
HABITS: The Pectoral Sandpiper is the champion migrant of the sandpiper world. Some birds that breed in the western Russian Arctic migrate east through Alaska to winter grounds in southern South America: a round trip of 30,000 km. On migration individual birds defend temporary feeding territories, as they forage in freshwater wetlands by pecking prey off the surface. Food includes fly larvae, beetles, crickets, grasshoppers, spiders, and snails. On the breeding grounds in the far North, males stake out a territory by flying at very slow speeds, low over the tundra, and inflating a special throat pouch. They make a deep, hooting noise as they advertise their presence. In contrast to many other sandpipers, the female builds the nest scrape alone on the male's territory. The male will mate with other females who enter his territory. Shortly after the female begins to incubate the four eggs, the male abandons her and migrates south. After a 21-23 day incubation period, the chicks hatch and immediately leave the nest to forage under the female's protection. The young birds depart for the long migration south about 4-6 weeks after hatching.
STATUS AND CONSERVATION: An uncommon fall migrant. Was more common in the 19th Century, but was heavily impacted by market hunting. Loss of wetland habitat at migration stopovers and on winter grounds may be an increasing threat.
RANGE: Breeds on the Arctic tundra from western Russia, across Siberia to coastal Alaska and northern Canada. Most birds winter in southern South America.

Willet
Catoptrophorus semipalmatus
Playero Aliblanco

IDENTIFICATION: A large, gray-brown shorebird, with a dramatic black and white wing pattern visible in flight. In non-breeding plumage the back is gray (see photo at upper left). Length: 33-41 cm.; weight: 173-375 g.

HABITAT: Mudflats, mangroves, and edges of ponds.

HABITS: Feeds on insects, crabs, small fish, molluscs and worms which it catches by pecking, probing in mud, or moving its bill back and forth in shallow water. As in many long-billed shorebirds, the tip of the Willet's bill is flexible, which aids in grabbing marine worms and other food deep in sand or mud. Also, like many shorebirds, it sometimes rests on one leg. The call is a very loud *"willet"*, or *"per-will-willet."* The nest is a shallow scrape in sand. Both sexes incubate the four eggs for 21-29 days, but the female sometimes abandons the male who then attends to the young for a few weeks after they hatch.

STATUS AND CONSERVATION: An uncommon migrant from North America with a few birds present in summer. Has recently bred in Puerto Rico.

RANGE: Breeds in the Bahamas and Greater Antilles, as well as in North America from New Brunswick south to Mexico, and in the northern Great Plains. Migrants from North America spend the winter as far south as coastal Brazil and Peru. Regular at Cabo Rojo.

American Oystercatcher   *Haematopus palliatus*   **Ostrero Americano**

A distinctive shorebird: dark brown and black above, and white below, with a bright, reddish-orange bill, and flesh-colored legs. In flight it has a contrasty, black and white wing pattern. Length: 40-44 cm.; weight: 400-700 g. It has a very narrow, chisel-shaped bill that is specialized for opening molluscs. It often cuts the hinge muscles of a clam or mussel with surgical precision, and then pries it open. Uncommon and local in Puerto Rico at rocky headlands and beaches, e.g. Desecheo, Vieques, Culebra and Cabezas de San Juan.

Stilt Sandpiper
Calidris himantopus
Playero Patilargo

IDENTIFICATION: A large shorebird with long greenish legs and a slight droop to the tip of the bill. In fall and winter, it is gray above, lighter below (bird at left is a juvenile molting into winter plumage). In breeding plumage it is barred with brown below and has a chestnut patch behind the eye. Length: 20-23 cm.; weight: 50-70 g.
HABITAT: Shallow pools in mangroves, salt flats, and estuaries.
HABITS: Takes advantage of its long legs and wades up to its belly in shallow pools. It alternately submerges and raises its head to probe the mud for worms, insects, molluscs, other invertebrates and seeds. This feeding movement looks like the action of a sewing machine.
STATUS AND CONSERVATION: A common winter visitor and migrant. Over 1,600 Stilt Sandpipers have been counted on one day in fall migration at Cabo Rojo's salt flats. However, the species is probably not common worldwide, and the total population may only be 50,000 breeding birds.
RANGE: Breeds on the tundra in a very narrow area of coastal plain in Alaska and far northern Canada. A regular location to find this species is in pools near Cabo Rojo.

Short-billed Dowitcher
Limnodromus griseus
Chorlo Pico Corto

A gray-brown shore bird with yellow-green legs. Despite its name, the Short-billed Dowitcher actually has a fairly long bill, somewhat thicker at the base, which it uses to probe deeply in mud for food. Length: 25-29 cm.; weight: 65-154 g. A common winter resident in wetlands on Puerto Rico, it breeds in Central Canada and southern Alaska.

Wilson's Snipe
Gallinago delicata
Becasina

A medium-sized shorebird, with a mottled brown-and-black body, dark stripes on the head, and a long bill. Length: 28 cm.; weight: 100 g. An uncommon winter resident in Puerto Rico, it inhabits grasslands and wet fields and breeds in much of northern North America. This bird is legally hunted, but is a challenge to shoot since it has an erratic flight pattern. Regular at Caño Tiburones Nature Reserve. Formerly called the Common Snipe.

Laughing Gull
Larus atricilla
Gaviota Gallega

IDENTIFICATION: The Laughing Gull has a different plumage in each of the first three years. The adult is white below and gray above, with black wing tips; in breeding plumage it has a black head and dull red bill. In winter plumage it lacks the black head, and the bill is black. In the first winter, the immature has a light gray back, brown wings and a broad black band at the end of the tail. Length: 39-46 cm.; weight: males 338 g., females 289 g.

HABITAT: Marshes, tidal flats, and coastal marine waters; also feeds at municipal garbage dumps and sewer outfalls, and follows fishing boats looking for scraps.

HABITS: Travels in flocks, and feeds on fish, plus crabs, worms and other marine invertebrates, snails, insects, and garbage. It plucks food off the surface of the water or surface dives. It sometimes lands on the back of a pelican to rob food from the side of its mouth, and will also chase terns to rob food in mid-air. In turn, the frigatebird robs food from the Laughing Gull. One of its calls sounds like a human laughing; it also has a high-pitched, begging call note when a flock is feeding. The nest is a grass-lined scrape on a vegetated beach, or shaded patch on a rocky island, sometimes near a colony of other seabirds. Both sexes incubate the 2-4 mottled greenish eggs for 24-28 days. Within a few days of hatching, young chicks can distinguish their parents' calls from other gulls.' Chicks move a short distance from the nest to seek shade, and are fed by the adults until two months of age. They fledge at 35-50 days but may stay in the nesting colony for several weeks afterwards.

STATUS AND CONSERVATION: The common gull of coastal Puerto Rico. This species was greatly reduced in the 19th Century due to hunting for feathers and eggs. Nests on isolated offshore rocky islands around Culebra, Cordillera Natural Reserve, Mona and Monito Islands. Only 5,000-10,000 pairs are estimated to breed in the West Indies.

RANGE: Breeds from Nova Scotia south throughout the Caribbean Basin, and also on the northwest coast of Mexico to Sonora. Northern breeders winter south to Peru and the mouth of the Amazon River. Common in Puerto Rico and adjacent islands, especially between April and September.

Black Tern
Chlidonias niger
Gaviota Ceniza

In breeding plumage, this small tern is dark gray with a black head and undersides, and a slightly forked tail (upper left photo). In fall migration and winter plumage, it is white below, with a white collar and a partial black hood. Length: 23-26 cm.; weight: 50-60 g. On migration through the Caribbean, flocks sometimes rest on beaches, pilings and mudflats, or forage on ponds and lagoons. It feeds on small fish, plankton and insects close to shore or at ponds. It winters at sea, often within a few kilometers of shore, but switches its habitat entirely when it nests on freshwater inland lakes and ponds in northern North America. An uncommon fall migrant in Puerto Pico. Population levels have declined dramatically in the 20th Century, probably due to the draining of wetlands in the breeding range. But pesticides are also a suspected cause of breeding failures. The Black Tern breeds in marshes of the northern USA and southern Canada. It winters off the Pacific coast of Central America, south to Peru, and from Panama east to the Guianas.

Gull-billed Tern
Sterna nilotica
Gaviota de Pico Corto, Gaviota Piquigorda

A relatively short, thick bill distinguishes this black-capped tern from its relatives. Length: 33-38 cm.; weight: 150-184 g. An uncommon visitor to Puerto Rico, mostly in summer months. It breeds along the coast in southern North America, the Bahamas and parts of the Old World. A Gull-billed Tern banded in Virginia was once recovered in Puerto Rico. Unlike other terns that feed mostly on fish, this species also eats crabs and chicks of other birds, and will hawk insects in the air, like a swallow.

Herring Gull   *Larus argentatus*   **Gaviota Argéntea**

A large, gray-backed gull with a thick bill, it goes through several plumage changes in the first four years, starting out as an all brown bird in the first year. Length: 56-66 cm.; weight: 800-1,250 g. It breeds in northern North America. Herring Gulls banded in Massachusetts and Michigan have been recovered in Puerto Rico. It is a regular visitor especially to San Juan, Arecibo and Mayagüez Harbors.

Royal Tern *Sterna maxima* **Gaviota Real**

IDENTIFICATION: The largest of the common tern species in Puerto Rico. It has a relatively thick orange bill and a short, forked tail. It has a black cap in breeding season (reduced to the nape most of the year). Length: 51 cm.; weight: 380-500 g.
HABITAT: Coastal marine waters.
HABITS: The Royal Tern dives for small fish, crabs, squid and shrimp. Sometimes it steals fish from other terns. During courtship, the male parades around the female, displaying his fish catch. Both sexes scrape a nest on a sandy beach in the nesting colony, often near other seabirds. Both sexes incubate a single, heavily-spotted, cream-colored egg (rarely two eggs in a clutch), and both feed the young. Often the young of a colony gather in a group called a creche. Despite the crowd, the parents can recognize their own young. Laughing Gulls prey on terns' nests.
STATUS AND CONSERVATION: Regularly seen between November and April in Puerto Rico, but only about 450-800 pairs actually nest in the Caribbean. North American migrants also winter in Puerto Rico. Birds banded in Maryland, Virginia, and the Carolinas have been recovered in Puerto Rico. The only confirmed breeding in Puerto Rico has been on rocky islands near Culebra, where up to 400 pairs have nested. Since 1988 those colonies have been reduced for unknown reasons to just a sporadic handful of pairs. Nest sites may have shifted to the Virgin Islands.
RANGE: Temperate and tropical coasts of West Africa and the Americas. Common winter visitor in San Juan Harbor, Laguna San José, Boquerón Bay, Mayagüez, and Laguna Torrecilla.

Ring-billed Gull
Larus delawarensis
Gaviota Piquianillada,
Gaviota Piquicerco

The Ring-billed Gull has a different plumage in each of the first three years. The adult is light gray on the back and upper wings, with black and white wing tips; the yellow bill has a black ring toward the tip. In the first winter

plumage, the immature has a light gray back, brown wings and sides, and a dull pink bill with a black tip. Length: 43 cm.; weight: 400-590 g. Feeds at beaches, bays and municipal garbage dumps. Nests on isolated islands in the northern interior of North America and migrates south in winter. Although uncommon in Puerto Rico, it is becoming more regular (San Juan Harbor and Mayagüez Bay). Birds banded in Ontario, Canada, have been recovered in Puerto Rico.

Sandwich Tern
Sterna sandvicensis
Gaviota de Pico Agudo

Has a black bill with a contrasting, yellow tip. It has a black cap in breeding season, but other times the black is limited to the back of the head. Unlike many medium-sized terns, its legs and feet are black. Length: 38 cm.; weight: 170-210 g. Forages in coastal marine waters; nests on isolated sandbars and islands. Often feeds, roosts and travels with Royal Terns. Both sexes incubate a single egg (occasionally two) and feed the young. A locally common breeder and winter migrant. Sandwich Terns banded in North Carolina have been recovered in Puerto Rico. Breeds in eastern North America and a few Caribbean islands and disperses as far south as Uruguay in winter. Nests at Culebra Island and some islets off La Parguera and Guayanilla. It is a regular winter visitor to San Juan harbor, Boquerón Bay, and Mayagüez Bay. A yellow-billed form, the Cayenne Tern, is sometimes considered a separate species (*Sterna eurygnatha*), and has bred at Culebra and La Parguera.

Roseate Tern
Sterna dougallii
Palometa

A white tern with a long, forked tail and orangish legs. It has a thin black bill with variable amounts of red at the base. In breeding plumage, it has a black cap and a pink tinge to the undersides. When not breeding, the forehead is white. Length: 33-41 cm.; weight: 100 g. Feeds over shallow reefs and sandy shoals close to shore. It also follows schools of predatory fish to capture small fish forced to the surface. Both sexes share in building a scrape nest on a beach; on Culebra they nest between boulders on cliffs. Both sexes incubate the clutch of 1-3 eggs for 22-24 days and then feed the young for about eight weeks---long after the young fledge at 22-30 days. After breeding, this tern disperses to sea as far as northern Brazil. It is listed by the federal government as a threatened species in Puerto Rico. It declined from feather collecting for women's clothing, egg collecting for markets, and nest predation by gulls. The world breeding population is only 40,000 pairs, with about 4,000-6,000 in the Caribbean. In the Americas, it breeds in the Caribbean and New England. Birds banded as far north as Maine have been recovered in Puerto Rico. Regular breeder off Culebra and the small, treeless islets south of La Parguera.

Least Tern
Sterna antillarum
Gaviota Pequeña, Gaviota Chica

IDENTIFICATION: Smallest nesting tern in Puerto Rico. It has a black cap, a bright yellow bill, orangish legs, and a light gray back. Length: 21-23 cm.; weight: 47-50 g.
HABITAT: Shallow coastal waters .
HABITS: Hovers before plunging for small fish, 2-9 cm. long. Breeds at three years of age. Female lays 2-3 eggs and incubates for 20-22 days.
STATUS AND CONSERVATION: Breeds in small numbers on undisturbed beaches. In migration, Least Terns from North America pass through the Caribbean en route to winter grounds in South America. During the 19th Century, hundreds of thousands were shot and their wing and tail feathers plucked for women's hats. Humans can trample the well-hidden eggs at colonies. Turnstones, Oystercatchers, crabs, as well as dogs, cats, rats and mongoose may prey on eggs, young and adults. In North America, it sometimes breeds on gravel-roofed buildings.
RANGE: Breeds from New England south to the West Indies. Winters off Central and South America, but it is not known where the Caribbean breeding population specifically winters.

Brown Noddy
Anous stolidus
Cervera

IDENTIFICATION: A dark seabird with a white cap fading toward the neck and a wedge-shaped tail. Length: 40-45 cm.; weight: 180 g.
HABITAT: Feeds both inshore and well off shore.
HABITS: Snatches squid and fish from the surface of the ocean or dives at a shallow angle. It spends much of its life at sea. Noddies can travel widely: One bird banded in Florida was recovered 12 years later in Puerto Rico. Noddies don't breed until 3-7 years of age. They nest on cliff ledges, trees and shrubs. Both sexes incubate the egg for alternating 24-hour periods over 33-36 days,
STATUS AND CONSERVATION: Common only in the waters off the nesting colonies. The Caribbean breeding population is estimated at 10,000-18,000 pairs, with about 1,000-1,500 pairs breeding near Culebra. Hurricane Hugo killed many birds at nesting colonies.
RANGE: Tropical waters worldwide. It nests in island colonies on or near Mona, Monito, and Culebra Islands, and Cordillera Natural Reserve.

Common Tern
Sterna hirundo
Gaviota Común, Charrán Común

A white tern with a long, forked tail. The red on the bill is usually more extensive than on the Roseate Tern, and the back is darker gray. The primary feathers have dark tips on the underside (light tips in the Roseate Tern). Length: 31-35 cm.; weight: 110-145 g. Uncommon migrant.

Bridled Tern
Sterna anaethetus
Gaviota Monja

IDENTIFICATION: Dark gray-brown above and white below, with a white collar, black cap, and white forehead. Length: 30-32 cm.; weight: 110-180 g.

HABITAT: Feeds at sea, often within 10 miles from shore.
HABITS: The Bridled Tern dips to the sea surface to catch small fish, usually less than 6 cm. long. It occasionally eats squid or crustaceans near the surface. It perches on floating wood, plastic or rafts of seaweed in the ocean, but often returns to land to sleep. In May and June this tern builds a scrape nest under the protection of vegetation or rocks, and lays a single egg. The incubation period is 28-30 days, and the chick fledges 50-65 days after hatching. Typically does not breed until it is four years old.
STATUS AND CONSERVATION: Locally common in coastal areas in the breeding season.
RANGE: Tropical oceans throughout the world, except the Central Pacific. Regularly seen during the breeding season in waters off the nesting colonies on Monito, Culebra and Mona Islands, the Cordillera Natural Reserve, and rocky offshore cays and cliff crevices between Isabela and Barceloneta.

Sooty Tern
Sterna fuscata
Gaviota Oscura

IDENTIFICATION: Black above and white below, with a white forehead. Blacker back and tail than in the Bridled Tern. Length: 36-45 cm.; weight: 200 g. See also photo on page 9.
HABITAT: Except when nesting, this bird is highly pelagic and seen only far from shore.
HABITS: Soars alone or sometimes with frigatebirds over the open ocean in search of schools of fish. It will hover over a school and then snatch a squid or fish (typically 6-8 cm. long) in a quick dive without entering the water. It may even catch a flying fish in mid-air, and sometimes feeds at night. In some regions, fishermen follow Sooty Terns as an indicator of productive fishing grounds. Like the frigatebird, its feathers cannot tolerate prolonged submersion in water, and some biologists theorize that it may sleep while flying. Unlike Sooty Terns elsewhere which nest on exposed ground, in Puerto Rico both sexes build a nest scrape in a colony near or under vegetation. The male and female incubate the single egg in 24-hour shifts and then feed the young for three weeks after they fledge. The Sooty Tern typically does not breed until 3-5 years of age.
STATUS AND CONSERVATION: Locally abundant during the breeding season from April to September. It has not been recorded between October and March. Although most individuals return to the same nesting sites (site tenacity), recruitment from other colonies as far as Florida has been documented. At least 14 predator species prey upon eggs, chicks or adults. Egg harvesting, although illegal, continues at the Culebra colonies.
RANGE: Tropical oceans throughout the world. Regularly seen off the nesting colonies on Culebra, Monito, and Mona Islands, and the Cordillera Natural Reserve during the breeding season.

Rock Pigeon
Columba livia
Paloma Común, Paloma Casera

IDENTIFICATION: The plumage of this bird in its native lands is dark gray with a white rump, and dark banding on the wings and tail tip. However, Rock Pigeons whose ancestors have recently escaped from captivity may have a variety of white, brown, gray, black and bluish colors that have been bred into captive varieties over the centuries. Length: 31-34 cm.; weight: 180-355 g.
HABITAT: City parks, buildings, streets, and fields near human habitation.
HABITS: Travels in flocks to preferred feeding grounds, and is often quite bold in city parks. The male displays by inflating its neck and strutting in front of the female. Wild Rock Pigeons nest in colonies on man-made structures, such as

churches, abandoned buildings, bridges, and store fronts, where they build a crude nest of sticks and other plant material. The Rock Pigeon mates for life. Although it lays only two eggs at a time, it may have up to five broods a year. Nest material and feces accumulate with each nesting, so that older nests can be 20 cm. high. The female incubates the eggs by night, the male by day. The incubation period is 16-19 days, and the young fledge 35-37 days after hatching.
STATUS AND CONSERVATION: Common, introduced species in urban areas. Rock Pigeons are kept by many hobbyists in Puerto Rico. The Rock Pigeon was domesticated about 5,000 years ago. It was used as a carrier pigeon to carry messages, and is still kept for food, racing, or show.
RANGE: Native to Europe and Asia, but now introduced worldwide in urban areas. Regular inhabitant of many town plazas throughout Puerto Rico. Formerly called Rock Dove.

White-crowned Pigeon
Patagioenas leucocephala
Paloma Cabeciblanca

IDENTIFICATION: The White-crowned Pigeon is dark, slate gray with a white cap. Immatures have a dull, gray cap. Length: 33-35 cm.; weight: 232-240 g.
HABITAT: Coastal forests, mangroves, and lower hills.
HABITS: Travels in small flocks, and forages for fruits among the branches of hardwood trees and palms, rather than on the ground as in most other pigeons. Although this species forages in low coastal forests, it can be hard to see well because it often flies like a terrain-hugging missile—flying up and down right above the treetops. At mid-day it rests by sitting still within the forest canopy. Both sexes share in building a shallow stick nest, lined with softer grasses. Both sexes incubate the 1-2 white eggs for 13-15 days. The male does most of the incubation during the day while the female incubates primarily at night. During the first few days after hatching, the nestlings are fed only pigeon's milk, which is rich in lipids and protein. Both parents gradually add fruit to the diet, until 2/3 of the diet is fruit at two weeks after hatching. The chicks fledge at 17-25 days. Will sometimes raise more than one brood per year. Birds travel extensively among islands: White-crowned Pigeons banded in the Bahamas and on St. Croix in the Virgin Islands have been recovered in Puerto Rico.
STATUS AND CONSERVATION: Now a very local, permanent resident in Puerto Rico. It was common and more widespread in the 19th Century, but hunting and destruction of coastal forests have reduced this species' population dramatically.
RANGE: Breeds from the Bahamas and the Florida Keys east to Antigua, and on islands off Central America. Regular locations to find this species include the grounds of the Dorado Beach Hotel, in the coastal forests near the Dorado public beaches and in the limestone hills between Bayamón and Vega Baja.

Scaly-naped Pigeon
Patagioenas squamosa
Paloma Turca

IDENTIFICATION: A dark gray pigeon with a dull purple head. At close range a bright red eye-ring is apparent. An outer eye ring can be either yellow-cream colored or white, depending on age and nutrition. Length: 32-41 cm.; weight: 250-326 g.
HABITAT: Moist forests.
HABITS: Feeds in trees on fruits, seeds, leaf buds, and snails. Despite its size, this pigeon hides effectively in trees and is usually seen only when it flies in the distance or is perched on a distant wire or tree limb. The typical song is a slow, booming, series of four notes with the last note more prolonged, "*who-hoo-hoo-hooo.*" It calls from January to July, with peak calling correlated with the fruiting of preferred tree species. The nest is a loose stick platform on a tree limb or in epiphytes. The female lays 1-2 white eggs. The incubation period is 14-15 days, with young fledging at 18-22 days. After breeding, this pigeon congregates in small groups at fruiting trees.
STATUS AND CONSERVATION: Common, permanent resident in mountain forests, where it has benefited from the recovery of native forests in the 20th Century. This is the most commonly shot pigeon of the four species legally hunted (typically September to November). Population levels decline after severe hurricanes, presumably due to temporary food scarcity.
RANGE: Breeds on most Caribbean islands, except the Bahamas and Jamaica. It is regularly heard in mountain forests, and is quite tame on Culebra where hunting is prohibited.

Plain Pigeon
Patagioenas inornata
Paloma Sabanera

IDENTIFICATION:: A large gray pigeon with wine-colored overtones. In flight a narrow white band is visible on the wing. At close range, its red feet and white eyes contrast with the plain plumage. Length: 39-41 cm.; weight: 250 g.

HABITAT: In the past, the Plain Pigeon utilized a wide variety of habitats including mountain forests, thorn scrub, mangroves and open country. Currently found mostly in moist mountain forests.

HABITS: The Plain Pigeon primarily forages in trees for fruits, berries, buds and flowers. Its favorite fruits include royal ralm (*Roystonea borinqena*), dama de día (*Cestrum diurnum*), matchwood (*Schefflera morototoni*), trumpet tree (yagrumo, *Cecropia schreberiana*), and camasey (*Miconia* sp.). It drinks water from the flowers of African tulip trees, bromeliads or droplets on leaves. The call consists of three, deep, cooing notes with the first being longer and more emphatic; also an *"urr"* growl when breeding; and a *"wet"* note when establishing territory. December-July is the main breeding period, although the Plain Pigeon may nest at any time of year. The stick nest is placed in a bamboo or hardwood tree with dense sheltering leaves, sometimes near nests of other Plain Pigeons. Typically the female lays one white egg, but may have three broods per year. Young fledge at 23 days. After breeding, the Plain Pigeon congregates in larger flocks for foraging and roosting.

STATUS AND CONSERVATION: This bird was a common species until the mid-19th Century, but is now on the federal endangered species list. Hunting and deforestation reduced its numbers dramatically until it was thought to be extinct. In 1958 a population was discovered near Cidra, and since then, pigeons have been located primarily at six locations: near Comerío, Caguas, Cayey, Aibonito, San Lorenzo, and Cidra. Plain Pigeons observed outside these areas should be reported to the Dept. of Natural Resources. The current population fluctuates at about 2,000 in the wild and 40-50 in a captive breeding program at the University of Puerto Rico/Humacao. This program had developed techniques that are models for captive breeding of other rare pigeon species around the world. For example, the program had used Ringed Turtle-Doves (*Streptopelia risoria*) to incubate Plain Pigeon eggs, but because the Plain Pigeon has a longer incubation period of 18 days, two synchronized Turtle-Doves had to be used to incubate the Plain Pigeon egg in a relay. Although release of captive birds has been tried to supplement the wild population, the primary strategy for restoring this species is to enforce the ban on hunting in Cidra, and enhance the protection of forest habitat. Ex-urban development in mountain areas is a major threat, as is nest predation by Pearly-eyed Thrashers, Red-legged Thrushes, and rats, as well as parasitism of chicks by fly maggots of *Philornis pici*. Scaly-naped Pigeons may force Plain Pigeons into marginal habitat for feeding and nesting. Hurricanes, such as Hurricane Hugo, are also a threat at the end of the breeding season. This species passed through a population "bottleneck" in the early 20th Century, so the genetic diversity of the surviving birds may be a long-term concern.

RANGE: Endemic to the Greater Antilles. A regular location to find the Plain Pigeon in Puerto Rico is in the trees around the baseball field at Escuela Intermedia Sabana near Comerío (PR 172, Km 1.5).

White-winged Dove
Zenaida asiatica
Tórtola Aliblanca, Aliblanca

IDENTIFICATION: A light brown, or gray-brown dove with red legs, a blue eye ring, and a striking white wing patch on the folded wing. Immature birds are duller and lack the blue eye ring (see photo below). In flight, the wing patch is visible from far away. Length: 25-31cm.; weight: 125-187 g.

HABITAT: Gardens, mangroves, and agricultural areas in moist zones of the island, but also common in dry scrub forest.

HABITS: Small flocks of this species forage on the ground and occasionally in trees for seeds and fruits. It is readily attracted to bird seed feeders, and will fight with other doves for the best feeding spots. The song has a variety of rhythms including "*who cooks for you.*" The White-winged Dove sometimes flicks its tail upward repeatedly when scared or when agitated by a rival bird. The male incorporates tail-raising in its courtship display, and fans the tail open and closed quickly to impress the female. Both sexes share in building a flimsy stick nest, lined with bark and leaves. The female lays two creamy or white eggs, which both sexes incubate for about 14 days. Young fledge at 13-16 days, but often only one chick survives. As with many dove species, the White-wing can disperse widely, with flocks migrating between islands. One bird banded in Santa Isabel in southern Puerto Rico was shot on Vieques the same year.

STATUS AND CONSERVATION: A common, permanent resident. This species is expanding its range and reached Puerto Rico in the mid-20th Century. It has benefited from agricultural alterations of the landscape. This is one of four species of doves legally hunted (September to November).

RANGE: Breeds from the southwestern USA, through Central America to Panama; and in the southern Bahamas and Greater Antilles. A typical location to find this species is at Guánica State Forest.

Zenaida Dove
Zenaida aurita
Tórtola
Cardosantera

IDENTIFICATION: A plump, brown pigeon with an iridescent purple patch on the neck. It has black spots and a white bar on the wings. The white outer feathers on its rounded tail, and the narrow, white trailing edge to the wings are striking in flight. Length: 28-30 cm.; weight: 120-180 g.
HABITAT: Farms, mangroves, open forests, and towns, especially in lowlands.

HABITS: Often seen on exposed perches such as treetops and electrical lines, or flying quickly over open fields. The wings make a whistling sound as the bird takes off. The Zenaida Dove walks on the ground searching for food, and will fly to streams and puddles for water early in the day. It sometimes feeds on fruits in trees, and is readily attracted to bird feeders near houses. It has been documented to feed on seeds and fruits of over 77 plant species in Puerto Rico, but occasionally eats ants, flies and earthworms. The song is commonly described as a mournful, "*cuacoo-coo-coo.*" Its nest is a crude stick platform placed in a cactus, royal palm, mango or other tree, and contains two white eggs. The incubation period is 13-15 days, and the young fledge about two weeks after hatching. Can produce three to five broods in one year. In most of Puerto Rico, the nesting season peaks in February to May, but it may nest at any time of year. As with many dove species, the Zenaida Dove can disperse widely. One bird banded in Juncos in eastern Puerto Rico was shot on Vieques in the same year.
STATUS AND CONSERVATION: A common species except in dense forest. It nested on the ground at one time (and still does so on Mona and Culebra Islands), but the introduced mongoose has restricted ground nesting by this bird, as well as other species. The Zenaida Dove has probably increased in numbers due to the clearing of forests in the last two centuries. It is one of four dove species legally hunted (September to November).
RANGE: This species occurs in the northern Yucatán Peninsula, and throughout the Caribbean islands, south to Grenada. It formerly occurred in the Florida Keys until extirpated by hunting and habitat destruction there.

Ringed Turtle-Dove
Streptopelia risoria
Paloma Collarina

IDENTIFICATION: Light gray below, with a light brown back and a pointed tail; this species has a black collar around the back of the neck. Length: 26 cm.; weight: 130 g.

HABITAT: Cities and towns, usually near houses.

HABITS: This species is often seen perched on wires, or foraging on streets or gardens near houses. It feeds on seeds and insects. The female lays 1-2 eggs, which are incubated for 14-15 days. Young fledge at 15 days.

STATUS AND CONSERVATION: A domesticated species that may breed in the wild.

RANGE: Over much of the world, farmers and hobbyists keep the Ringed Turtle-Dove as a pet, or for food. It is regularly seen at La Parguera in that area. Some taxonomists do not consider this a separate species, but rather the domesticated form of the African Collared-Dove (*Streptopelia roseogrisea*). The wild form of the African Collared-Dove is native to northern sub-Sahara Africa and the Arabian Peninsula. The larger Eurasian Collared Dove, (*Streptopelia decaocto*) was introduced to the Bahamas from Europe, and has spread rapidly into southeastern North America over the late 20th Century, with recent sightings in Puerto Rico.

Mourning Dove
Zenaida macroura
Tórtola Rabilarga

IDENTIFICATION: A medium-sized dove with a long, pointed tail, especially obvious in flight. It lacks the white wing patches and deeper reddish hues of the Zenaida Dove. Length: 23-34 cm. with males tending to be longer; weight: 108 g.

HABITAT: Open country with occasional trees, especially near agricultural fields or farmyards.

HABITS: The Mourning Dove feeds almost exclusively on the ground where it bobs its head as it walks in search of plant seeds and waste grain in fields. It flies to a pond or open puddle in the morning and late in the afternoon to quickly drink. The song is a series of cooing notes, very similar to the Zenaida Dove's song, but often with a slower ending. The Dove's English name reflects the "sad" quality of the song. As breeding season approaches, mates preen each other's feathers (allopreening), and the male performs a circling display flight, with wings held stiffly downward. The female weaves a crude nest platform in a tree fork, and lays two white eggs in a clutch. Both sexes incubate the eggs over a 13-14 day period, with the female preferring to incubate at night. Only 12-14 days after hatching, the young are ready to fly. Adults may raise additional broods later in the season. After nesting is completed, this species forms feeding flocks of dozens or hundreds of birds.

STATUS AND CONSERVATION: A common, local species, especially in the southwest. It expanded its range into Puerto Rico in the 20th Century, and is now common enough that it is one of four species of doves legally hunted. Doves suffer from lead poisoning after eating lead shot they find in fields.

RANGE: Breeds from southern Canada to southern Mexico, the Bahamas and Greater Antilles. In winter, North American breeders migrate as far south as Costa Rica. A regular location to find this species is in open fields near Laguna Cartagena National Wildlife Refuge.

Common Ground-Dove   *Columbina passerina*   **Rolita**

IDENTIFICATION: A tiny, gray dove, with a scaly pattern on the head and breast. The rufous wings are striking in flight. Length: 15-18 cm.; weight: 22-42 g.

HABITAT: Farms, open country and towns.

HABITS: Bobs its head vigorously as it walks in fields, grassy roadsides, and even city streets looking for seeds and berries. It is easily attracted to bird feeders, where it protects the best feeding spots by flashing its bright rufous wing linings to scare off rivals of its own species, and sometimes other birds as well. When flushed it flies a short distance, then hides in shrubs or grass. The song is a rising "*woo-ah*," repeated persistently at any time of day, but especially at dawn. Calling peaks between April and June. Pairs travel together throughout the year. Before mating, the pair vigorously bob their heads up and down while moving from one perch to a n o t h e r. The nest is a flat, stick platform in a tree, palm, or sometimes a depression in the ground. It even nests on top of air conditioners or roofs. The nest contains two white eggs. Both sexes incubate the eggs for 13-14 days, and feed the young until fledging 11-13 days after hatching. Like other doves, its crop produces pigeon's milk, a thick secretion for feeding its chicks. May have several broods in one year.

STATUS AND CONSERVATION: Abundant in open country at mid- to lower elevations, where it has adapted to urbanization. It is more common now than two centuries ago due to clearing of forests.

RANGE: Occurs from the southern USA, through the Caribbean islands, to Ecuador and southern Brazil. There are 18 subspecies, one of which (*Columbina passerina portoricensis*) is unique to Puerto Rico and the Virgin Islands. It is smaller and more heavily scaled than North American subspecies. Another (*Columbina passerina exigua*), inhabits Mona Island.

Key West Quail-Dove
Geotrygon chrysia
Paloma Perdiz Grande, Perdiz Áurea, Paloma Perdiz Áurea

IDENTIFICATION: Bright, reddish-brown above, gray below, with a dramatic, white horizontal stripe below the eye. The back of the neck is iridescent green, and the back is iridescent purple. Length: 27 - 31 cm.; weight: 148 -199 g.
HABITAT: Dense native forests, especially dryer forests with a shrub layer.
HABITS: Forages on the forest floor for berries, seeds, and occasionally snails. Quail-Doves walk slowly, bobbing the head forward and backward as they walk. The rustling of leaves is often the first clue that one is nearby. When frightened, it will quickly run into dense undergrowth, or fly a short distance. Sings a single, fading note in June and July. The nest is a flimsy platform of twigs low in a tree or in a tangle of vines. The female lays two buff-colored eggs.
STATUS AND CONSERVATION: An uncommon, permanent resident. The recovery of native forest in the 20th Century has probably helped this species. It was formerly hunted.
RANGE: The West Indies, formerly the Florida Keys. Regular at Laguna Tortuguero Nature Reserve and Susúa State Forest.

Bridled Quail-Dove
Geotrygon mystacea
Perdiz de Martinica
Paloma Perdiz Bigotuda

Smaller than the Key West Quail-Dove, with duller upperparts, and buffy undersides. Iridescent purple on the neck and upper back. Length: 24-30 cm.; weight: 230 g. Rare and local in Puerto Rico, but colonized the island only recently. Breeds on islands of the eastern Caribbean. Regularly reported from Vieques.

Ruddy Quail-Dove
Geotrygon montana
Paloma Perdiz Pequeña
Paloma Perdiz Rojiza

Reddish-brown above, and rufous below, with a buff line below the eye. Female is duller. Length: 19-28 cm.; weight: 85-152 g. Its low-pitched *"coo"* note is heard in late spring and summer. Breeds from Mexico through the Caribbean to Brazil. Often seen flying across mountain roads and in dense forests with a well-developed understory and in shade coffee and citrus groves. Common at Maricao and Carite State Forests.

Monk Parakeet
Myiopsitta monachus
Perico Monje

IDENTIFICATION: Mostly green, with a gray throat and forehead, and a long, narrow tail. It appears dark in flight except for the grayish throat. Length: 28 cm.; weight: 90-140 g.

HABITAT: City parks, gardens and farms.

HABITS: Travels in small noisy flocks. It feeds on palm nuts, fruits, grain, seeds, and some flowers, buds and insects. It is the only parrot species in the world that builds a huge, communal stick nest.

STATUS AND CONSERVATION: This common, introduced bird is considered an agricultural pest in its homeland. The Monk Parakeet is one of many parrots and parakeets that have escaped or been intentionally released in Puerto Rico. Although this particular species is common in its native land, many other species of parrots and parakeets are endangered. See also the endangered, Puerto Rican Parrot on page 13.

RANGE: Native to South America. Common in parks in Old San Juan.

White-winged Parakeet   *Brotogeris versicolurus*
Periquito de Ala Blanca, Periquito Aliamarillo

IDENTIFICATION: A widespread, introduced parakeet, the White-winged Parakeet is bright green, with a long, thin tail, a light-colored bill, and dramatic, yellow-and-white wing patches. It was formerly called the Canary-winged Parakeet. Length: 22-25 cm.; weight: 62-81 g.

HABITAT: City parks, gardens and farms.

HABITS: Parakeets travel in flocks to feed on fruits and seeds. They rest in treetops in mid-day where they can be heard, but are often difficult to see. This species nests inside termite nests where the female lays 4-6 eggs per clutch. Young fledge about 4-5 weeks after hatching.

STATUS AND CONSERVATION: Common in lowland Puerto Rico where it was first imported from Venezuela about 1916. About 230,000 were legally imported to the USA between 1968 and 1972. Many other parrots and parakeets have been introduced to Puerto Rico but are not as widespread or well-established as the White-winged or Monk Parakeets.

RANGE: Native to the Amazon River basin from southeastern Colombia and northeastern Peru to northeastern Brazil and French Guiana.

Mangrove Cuckoo
Coccyzus minor
Pájaro Bobo Menor

IDENTIFICATION: A slender bird with buffy or light yellow underparts, a gray cap, and a black facial mask. It has a long tail with prominent white spots. Its bill is slightly curved. Length: 33 cm.; weight: 65 g. See also the endemic Puerto Rican Lizard-Cuckoo on page 14.

HABITAT: Thick vegetation in mangroves, coastal scrub, mountain forests, limestone hills, and coffee plantations, especially at middle or lower altitudes.

HABITS: The Mangrove Cuckoo, like other members of its family, moves deliberately in thickets and tangles looking for caterpillars, grasshoppers, crickets, cicadas, spiders, and insect larvae, as well as frogs, lizards, snails, berries, and the eggs and nestlings of small birds. It is one of the few birds that eats hairy caterpillars, and sometimes the stomach is lined with caterpillar spines stuck in the stomach wall. Although quite common, the Mangrove Cuckoo is sometimes difficult to see because of its slow movements, unless it reveals its location by calling. However, it seems relatively unafraid of humans, and will often allow close approach. The song is a series of 8-20, low-pitched, resonant notes that sound like an electric guitar. Its nest is a thin twig platform on a horizontal limb and contains 2-3 blue-green eggs.

STATUS AND CONSERVATION: A common, permanent resident in thickets and forests.

RANGE: Occurs from southern Florida through most of the Antilles, and from Mexico and Central America, south to the Amazon basin. Regular at Guánica and Vega State Forests.

Yellow-billed Cuckoo
Coccyzus americanus
Pájaro Bobo Pechiblanco

White undersides and chestnut wing patches are striking in flight. Lacks the Mangrove Cuckoo's black eye mask. Length: 26-30 cm.; weight: 55-65 g. Uncommon nester, with some winter migrants from North America.

Smooth-billed Ani
Crotophaga ani
Judío, Garrapatero

IDENTIFICATION: An all-black bird with a long tail and a high, ridged bill that gives it the appearance of a black parrot. Length: 30-36 cm.; weight: males 115 g., females 95 g.
HABITAT: Open country with scattered trees; open forests, bushy fields, hedgerows, and pastures, even vacant city lots.
HABITS: Hops or runs in small flocks on the ground, in bushes or trees, eating insects, lizards, berries and other birds' eggs. They often sit in the open, on branches or fence lines, huddled close together and occasionally preening their neighbor's feathers. Anis sometimes perch on the ground or a branch and hold the wings out to catch the sun or dry out after a rain. Calls include a rising squawk. Several pairs defend a territory and construct a large stick nest where the females lay their blue eggs and incubate the eggs together. One nest near Aguadilla contained twenty eggs in layers.
STATUS AND CONSERVATION: A common, easy to observe species.
RANGE: Occurs in the West Indies, south Florida, parts of Central America, and most of lowland South America to northern Argentina.

Short-eared Owl   *Asio flammeus*   **Múcaro Real**

IDENTIFICATION: The Short-eared Owl has a big-headed look, and flies on long wings that are lighter below, with a dark mark on the forewing. Length: 34-42 cm.; weight: 325 g. See also the smaller, endemic Puerto Rican Screech-Owl on page 15.
HABITAT: Fields, pastures, marshes and woodland clearings.
HABITS: This owl has a deep, slow wing beat as it flies at dawn and dusk, low over grasslands in search of small mammals, lizards, and birds. It often hovers over a single spot, like a Kestrel, and will sometimes feed in daylight. It regurgitates pellets of undigested bones and fur.
STATUS AND CONSERVATION: Uncommon, permanent resident in Puerto Rico. Conversion of forests to grasslands helped this species, but the introduced mongoose and the conversion of farmland to development have reduced habitat. This low-flying owl often collides with cars and wires.
RANGE: Breeds in North America and the Greater Antilles. The smaller and darker subspecies in the Caribbean, including Puerto Rico's *Asio flammeus portoricensis,* have been proposed as a separate species from North American forms. Regular locations to find this species are in open country near Salinas and Caño Tiburones Nature Reserve.

Antillean Nighthawk
Chordeiles gundlachii
Querequequé

IDENTIFICATION: A mottled-gray, long-winged bird, with a buffy tinge to the undersides. A white band on each wing is obvious in flight. The male has a white tail band. Length: 20-21 cm.; weight: 65 g. See also the endemic Puerto Rican Nightjar on page 16.

HABITAT: Open country, coasts, agricultural fields, pastures, and limestone forests.

HABITS: This species is one of the few land birds that breeds in Puerto Rico in the summer but migrates south for the winter. It arrives in April and departs in September. At twilight the nighthawk darts back and forth over open country, catching insects, such as beetles, flies, mosquitoes, moths, and flying ants. Its wide mouth is well-adapted to seizing prey in mid-air. Its nasal, three-note call, has a rhythm like its Spanish name, "*Querequequé*." The nighthawk is so well camouflaged that it is hard to see when perched on the ground---until it takes off. After arriving in the spring, the male has a dramatic courtship display in which he repeatedly dives from high in the air and pulls up just before reaching the ground. The nest is a scrape in gravel or sand. The nighthawk often nests on flat, gravel-roofed buildings in shopping malls and factories where it is safe from ground predators. The female lays one, sometimes two eggs and incubates them for about 19 days. The chick is precocious and can leave the nest within hours of hatching.

STATUS AND CONSERVATION: A summer resident in Puerto Rico. The introduced mongoose has probably affected this species, but clearing of forests in the 19th Century may have opened up habitat for the nighthawk. See also the endemic Puerto Rican Nightjar on page 16.

RANGE: Breeds from the Florida Keys, the Bahamas and Cuba east to the Virgin Islands. Most likely winters in South America. Regular at Cabo Rojo, and over many shopping malls.

Antillean Mango
Anthracothorax dominicus
Zumbador Dorado,
Colibrí Dorado, Zunzún

IDENTIFICATION: A large hummingbird with a curved bill. The male is green above with an iridescent green throat, black breast and grayish abdomen, and an iridescent purple tail. The female is green above and white below, with a white-tipped tail. The brightness and color of the feathers depend on the sun's angle. Immature males resemble females, but have a black line down the middle of the white breast. Length: 11-12 cm.; weight: 4.0-8.2 g. See also the similar, endemic Green Mango on page 17.

HABITAT: Gardens and forest edges.

HABITS: Feeds on insects (small wasps, ants, beetles, flies, and homopterous insects), spiders, and flower nectar. The Antillean Mango will come to sugar water feeders, but may take many months to discover the feeder. Hummingbirds can hover by rotating their wings in a "figure 8" pattern, generating lift in both forward and backward directions. They beat their wings at more than 20 strokes per second. To accomplish this, the breast muscles are large, constituting almost 30% of the bird's body weight. Despite its small size, the Mango and other hummingbirds drive out merlins, kestrels, kingbirds, woodpeckers, and other larger birds that the hummingbird perceives as a threat in its territory. The Mango's tiny nest is made of vegetable fibers, covered with flecks of bark and lichen and bound together with spider webs. The female lays two white eggs. Although usually found in trees or banana plants 1-7 meters above the ground, the nest can be placed in odd locations like power lines, TV antennae, fences, and boat masts. The Mango may nest more than once a year, and nests are sometimes reused. Most nesting occurs from March to August, but it can nest at any time of year. Incubation period is about 15 days, with chicks fledging 22-25 days after hatching.

STATUS AND CONSERVATION: Commonest of the hummingbirds in Puerto Rico along the coast. It can be attracted to plantings of flowering plants.

RANGE: Occurs in Puerto Rico, Hispaniola and the Virgin Islands. A typical site to find this species is the grounds of the Botanical Gardens in Río Piedras. Of interest, Puerto Rico has five species of resident hummingbirds, more than on any other West Indian island.

Green-throated Carib
Eulampis holosericeus
Zumbador de Pecho Azul
Zumbador Pechiazul

IDENTIFICATION: A large hummingbird with a downward curved bill. Both sexes have similar plumage: green above, with a black belly and a brilliant, iridescent green throat and breast. The lower border of the breast has a thin blue line, visible in the right light angle. The female's bill is somewhat longer and more curved. Length: 10-12 cm.; weight: 4.9-7.8 g.
HABITAT: Forests, mangroves, and gardens.
HABITS: Feeds on nectar, insects (flies, small wasps, lantern flies, leafhoppers, beetles), and spiders. It is readily attracted to sugar water feeders which it defends against Bananaquits. It sometimes catches insects in the air. The call is described as a harsh "*chewp*." This species typically breeds from March to July but can nest at other times. The female builds a well-hidden nest in a dense shrub or low in a tree. The nest is constructed of bark, lichens, and leaves, with a soft interior lining of downy plant fibers and feathers. The female lays two white eggs and does all the incubation and caring for the nestlings.
STATUS AND CONSERVATION: Common, but local, resident of Puerto Rico. It starred on a 32-cent US postage stamp (1998 Tropical Bird stamp series # 445915).
RANGE: Has been reported from much of lowland Puerto Rico, but typically breeds in eastern Puerto Rico, Culebra, and Vieques, east to Barbados. This is the common large hummingbird on Culebra and Vieques. Recently this species has been found near the entrance to the Parque Lineal in San Juan's Parque Central, and on the grounds of hotels on Vieques and Culebra.

Vervain Hummingbird
Mellisuga minima
Zumbador Verbena, Zumbaflor

The smallest bird ever documented in Puerto Rico, this species is white below and iridescent green above. Length: 6 cm.; weight: 2.2-3.6 g. Hovers with its tail cocked up. When flying by, it can be confused with a beetle or other large insect. Endemic to Jamaica and Hispaniola. Accidental in Puerto Rico.

Antillean Crested Hummingbird
Orthorhyncus cristatus
Zumbadorcito Crestado

IDENTIFICATION: The male and female have very different plumages. The male is green above and dark below, with an iridescent green crest that it erects when agitated or displaying. In contrast, the female lacks the crest, and is a dull, light gray underneath. The bill is straight and relatively short. Length: 8-10 cm.; weight: 2.0-4.3 g. See also the endemic Puerto Rican Emerald on page 18.

HABITAT: Forest understory and gardens.

HABITS: Feeds on insects (ants, beetles, small wasps), spiders, and nectar. The call is described as a double note—"*pit-chew*." The male of this species, like many other hummingbirds, has an aerial courtship display. He flashes his bright green crest in front of the perched female, as he flies back and forth in a tight arc in front of her. Nesting can occur at any time of year. The female builds a nest of leaves, bark, ferns and spider webs, placed low in a tree. She lays two white eggs and does all the incubation for 15 days. The young fledge at about three weeks of age.

STATUS AND CONSERVATION: The common small hummingbird of eastern Puerto Rico.

RANGE: Breeds from eastern Puerto Rico, Culebra, and Vieques, east to Grenada. Regular at the Humacao Nature Reserve.

Belted Kingfisher
Ceryle alcyon
Martín Pescador
Pájaro del Rey

IDENTIFICATION: The kingfisher has blue upper parts with a white collar. The underparts are white with a blue breast band. The female has an additional rusty-brown breast band below the blue one. The bill is large and stout, and the bird often raises its crest, giving it a big-headed appearance. When flying, it can be recognized from a distance by bursts of wingbeats. Length: 28-35 cm.; weight: 140-170 g. See also the endemic Puerto Rican Tody on page 19.

HABITAT: Ponds, lagoons, rivers and ocean shores: wherever the water is clear enough to see fish just below the surface.

HABITS: The kingfisher perches on exposed tree branches, wires, or posts over water. Both sexes defend a feeding territory against other kingfishers. The kingfisher dives for prey either directly from its perch or after briefly hovering. It uses its stout bill to catch fish, crustaceans, aquatic insect larvae, and sometimes even lizards or small birds and mammals. Most of its fish are less than 10 cm. long and are caught within 60 cm. of the water's surface. It regurgitates pellets with undigested bones and fish scales. Its call is a rattly, "*klek*" note, usually repeated in a long series. The Belted Kingfisher nests in North America in a 1-2 meter long burrow that both sexes dig in a mud bank. Sometimes even sand dunes or sawdust piles have been used as nest sites. Two of the kingfisher's toes are partially fused together, which aids in shoveling earth for the nest burrow. The nest chamber contains 6-7 white eggs. Over a 22-24 day period both sexes incubate the 6-7 white eggs. In the first few days after the eggs hatch, the parents

regurgitate digested food, but as the chicks grow, the parents gradually bring larger fish. The young birds defecate against the wall of the nest chamber, but then cover the feces with dirt from the burrow wall. The chicks leave the nest 27-29 days after hatching. The adults gradually reduce the feeding schedule and then entice the young to leave the nest by perching just outside the nest entrance while holding a fish in the bill. For the first few weeks after leaving the nest, the parents feed the young and teach them to fish by dropping prey in the water for the young to chase.

STATUS AND CONSERVATION: Common winter visitor, although a few non-breeding individuals linger throughout the year. In the kingfisher's breeding range, human activities such as the creation of reservoirs and gravel pits may have increased breeding opportunities.

RANGE: Breeds over most of North America. It retreats from most of its northern breeding range in winter and heads as far south as the West Indies and northwestern South America. A regular location in winter is at La Parguera.

Caribbean Elaenia   *Elaenia martinica*   Juí Blanco

IDENTIFICATION: A small flycatcher with a dull brown back, faint yellow belly, and two white wing bars. The wingbars and belly fade in worn plumage. When excited, it raises its crest, revealing a white central crown stripe. Often sits in an upright posture on tree branches. Length: 16-17 cm.; weight: 22 g. See also the endemic Puerto Rican Flycatcher on page 21.

HABITAT: Forest understory trees, especially arid scrub forests.

HABITS: Calls persistently in the breeding season early in the year from a perch in middle levels of the forest. The call consists of three whistled notes, rising in the middle; also a longer dawn song, "*Peweer-peweer-peweer.*" It often changes perches as it looks for insects (caterpillars, weevils, other beetles, earwigs) and spiders. Although it is in the flycatcher family, much of its diet consists of fruit. In one study in March and April, 86% of the stomach contents consisted of fruits; and some birds had no insects at all in their stomachs. The Elaenia aggressively chases others of its species from its territory. The nest is a cup in a forked tree branch, and typically contains 2-3 eggs.

STATUS AND CONSERVATION: A common forest species. It was first reported in Puerto Rico in 1963, and has become more common since then.

RANGE: Breeds in the Cayman Islands, the islands off the Yucatán Peninsula, some of the Bahama Islands; and from Puerto Rico east through the islands of the eastern Caribbean. Regular in the arid forests at Boquerón Nature Reserve and Guánica State Forest.

Gray Kingbird   *Tyrannus dominicensis*   Pitirre

IDENTIFICATION: Gray above and white below, with a black mask over the eyes. The tail has a slightly forked tip. A few red crown feathers are rarely visible. Length: 22-25 cm.; weight: 42-48 g.

HABITAT: Open country, parks, forest edges, and city streets: anywhere there is a perch and open areas to catch insects in the air.

HABITS: The common call is one of the most characteristic sounds of Puerto Rico. It sounds like its Spanish name, *"Pitirre."* The kingbird is one of the first birds to start singing before dawn, when it has a more prolonged, rolling, dawn song. It sits on an exposed perch, such as a dead branch, roof top, antenna, or telephone wire, and catches insects in flight or sometimes by gleaning insects off leaves. A sharp snapping noise can sometimes be heard when the bill closes on an insect. Insect prey include flies, dragonflies, wasps, bees, weevils, other beetles, caterpillars, and occasionally crickets and grasshoppers. Will also eat lizards, and has been reported to capture a small hummingbird. On average, about 1/5 of the diet consists of fruits and berries, which it typically grabs while hovering in front of, or below, the fruit. The kingbird sometimes feeds at night on insects attracted to streetlights. It is very aggressive---especially during the breeding season---toward neighboring pairs, as well as potential predators like hawks, falcons, egrets, gulls, cats, or humans. In fact, a popular expression is "cada guaraguao tiene su pitirre" which means, "every hawk has its kingbird" [pestering it]. The Latin name for the genus, *Tyrannus*, refers to this tyrannical behavior. Starting in January, pairs engage in an

aerial courtship flight. The kingbird lays 2-5 pink, mottled eggs in a stick nest on a shrub, small tree, antenna or pole, but often only two chicks will survive. Outside the breeding season, kingbirds use communal roosts in mangroves, bamboo thickets or trees in municipal plazas, where hundreds sometimes gather.

STATUS AND CONSERVATION: One of the commonest birds in Puerto Rico, the Gray Kingbird has adapted well to human settlement.

RANGE: Nests from coastal Georgia and Florida through the Caribbean islands to northern Colombia and Venezuela.

96

Loggerhead Kingbird
Tyrannus caudifasciatus
Clérigo

IDENTIFICATION: Similar to the Gray Kingbird, but with a browner back, a blackish upper head, and a yellow crown stripe (rarely visible). Length: 23-25 cm.; weight: 37 g.
HABITAT: Forest clearings and edges; shade coffee plantations.
HABITS: Perches in a clump of leaves or epiphytes, or on an exposed branch or wire near a forest clearing. It sallies out to catch insects in mid-air or snatch them from leaves. It also eats frogs and lizards. It sometimes hovers to eat seeds and berries, which compose a quarter of its diet. Insect prey include crickets, locusts, weevils, other beetles, moths, wasps, bugs (*Hemiptera*), and caterpillars. The song is a loud, bubbly, "*pi ti tity*", but outside the breeding season it vocalizes less often than the Gray Kingbird. Like the Gray Kingbird, the members of a pair will often greet each other just as one bird returns to a perch near the other. The Loggerhead Kingbird builds a loose cup nest of grass, seedpods, string, and other fibers. The female lays 2-4 eggs in a clutch.

STATUS AND CONSERVATION: A common, permanent resident in Puerto Rico. The restoration of forests in the late 20th Century has probably helped this species.
RANGE: Breeds in the northern Bahamas, the Cayman Islands, and the Greater Antilles. Regular in forest clearings at Maricao State Forest. The subspecies on Puerto Rico (*Tyrannus caudifasciatus taylori*) has a dark tail tip (light tail tip on other islands).

Lesser Antillean Pewee (Puerto Rican Pewee)   *Contopus latirostris*   **Bobito**

IDENTIFICATION: A small flycatcher with an olive-brown back, buffy underparts and two faint buff wing bars. Immature birds are duller (photo at left). Length: 15 cm.; average weight: 11.6 g.

HABITAT: Mountain forests, coffee plantations, and coastal scrub forests.

HABITS: Sits quietly upright on branches in the forest understory or a forest clearing. It quickly flies out to hover in front of a leaf to glean an insect ("sally-hover") or catch one in mid-air before returning to its perch. Its wide bill is adapted for flycatching. It will use one perch for multiple sorties, and then try out another perch for a while. Unlike many other flycatcher species in Puerto Rico, the pewee eats very little vegetable matter: 99% of its diet consists of insects and spiders. The pewee will allow close approach by humans, but may be hard to locate since it is less active than other flycatchers. The pewee is sometimes the key bird in mixed-species foraging flocks. Its nest is a cup on a tree limb and contains 2-3 eggs.

STATUS AND CONSERVATION: A common, but local species that is dependent on forest cover. It has adapted well to shade-grown coffee plantations.

RANGE: Occurs in central and western Puerto Rico, and in Guadeloupe, Dominica, Martinique and St. Lucia. Regular at Boquerón Nature Reserve and Maricao State Forest. The Puerto Rican subspecies (*Contopus latirostris blancoi*) is sufficiently different in plumage and song that taxonomists may eventually split the Puerto Rican form into a separate, endemic species, the Puerto Rican Pewee (*Contopus portoricensis*).

Black-whiskered Vireo
Vireo altiloquus
Julián Chiví

IDENTIFICATION: A small forest bird with an olive colored back, a thick bill, and black lines both through the eye and just below the bill (the "whisker"). Length: 15-17 cm.; weight: 18-20 g. See also the endemic Puerto Rican Vireo on page 22.
HABITAT: Forests, mangroves, and gardens.
HABITS: This vireo moves slowly through the forest canopy and vine tangles, so it is often difficult to locate. It gleans insects off leaves, sometimes hovering to pluck an insect. It also eats spiders, frogs, and many berries. Insects documented in its diet in Puerto Rico include caterpillars, mantids, walking sticks, grasshoppers, cicadas, weevils, other beetles, bugs, wasps, and ants. But over half the food in one study consisted of fruits and berries. The song is a monotonous repetition that sounds like its name in Spanish; also utters a frequent, scolding note. The female builds a basket-shaped nest on a forked limb and lays 2-3 white eggs with scattered brown or purple spots. The female does the incubation, but both sexes feed the chicks (middle photo). Often only one chick survives. The vireo can be located in May and June by tracking down the begging calls of chicks. Most birds arrive in February and March and depart for the winter in August, although a few birds spend the entire year in Puerto Rico.
STATUS AND CONSERVATION: A common summer resident in Puerto Rico. The restoration of forests in the 20th Century has probably helped this species.
RANGE: Breeds from the Florida coast south through the Caribbean islands. Winters in the lowlands of Venezuela, the Guianas, eastern Colombia and northwestern Brazil. Found in forests throughout the island; a regular place to find this species is at Maricao State Forest.

White-eyed Vireo *Vireo griseus* Vireo Ojiblanco

A small, shy bird, with yellow sides, two white wing bars, and a yellow "spectacle" around the white eye. Length:11-13 cm.; weight: 10-13 g. Breeds in the eastern USA and northeastern Mexico. Uncommon winter visitor in thickets and vine tangles, e.g., in Dorado and at the Caño Tiburones Nature Reserve.

Caribbean Martin
Progne dominicensis
Golondrina de Iglesias

IDENTIFICATION: A large swallow with a forked tail. It is dark iridescent blue with a white belly. The female and immatures have a smoky brown breast. Length: 17-20 cm.; weight: 42 g.
HABITAT: Towns and open country, often near water.
HABITS: Perches on wires or branches to rest, but is often seen flying over fields, pastures and towns, foraging for insects (flies, wasps, stinkbugs, dragonflies, termites, and beetles) and spiders. Makes a low-pitched, twangy note, often given in flight. It nests in single pairs or small colonies in old woodpecker holes or other cavities in palms, trees, cliffs, buildings, or even traffic lights. Thirty pairs were once recorded nesting in crevices in one chimney in Quebradillas. There are 4-6 white eggs in a clutch.
STATUS AND CONSERVATION: A common resident for much of the year in Puerto Rico. Most martins leave Puerto Rico from late September through December when they migrate to an unknown winter home, presumably in South America. The martin has probably benefited from nest sites that human construction offers. This species competes for nest boxes with the endangered Yellow-shouldered Blackbird. Wildlife biologists often put up extra nest boxes near blackbird nesting colonies to lure martins away.
RANGE: Nests on most Caribbean islands south to Tobago.

Barn Swallow
Hirundo rustica
Golondrina de Horquilla

Iridescent blue above, with a rusty throat and forehead. The long, deeply-forked tail is a prominent feature in flight. Length: 17-20 cm.; weight: 17-21 g. Forages over wetlands, fields, and coastal areas, often over water. Frequently flocks with Cave Swallows. In the breeding season in North America, females favor males with the longest and most symmetrical tail feathers. A common migrant visitor and uncommon winter resident in Puerto Rico. Breeds across the temperate zone of the Northern Hemisphere. Has recently expanded its breeding range in southeastern

North America to Florida. Winters from Panama and the West Indies, south to southern Argentina and Chile. Can be seen over El Morro in Old San Juan in migration.

Cave Swallow   *Petrochelidon fulva*   **Golondrina de Cuevas**

IDENTIFICATION: A square-tailed swallow, blue-gray above with a chestnut-colored rump and forehead. Length: 12-14 cm.; Weight: 19 g.
HABITAT: Farms, beaches, mangroves, open country, marshes, and towns.
HABITS: The Cave Swallow, singly or in loose flocks of several dozen birds, can be seen throughout the day feeding on airborne insects. Nests in colonies in caves, sea cliffs, and sinkholes, under bridges and on ledges of buildings. It builds a globular nest by scooping up mud from puddles or stream banks, and dabbing the mud on a ledge, one bill-full at a time. The nest may be used from one year to the next. The female lays 3-4 white eggs with brown spots. She does most of the incubation of the eggs, but the male helps feed the chicks.
STATUS AND CONSERVATION: A common, permanent resident.
RANGE: Breeds from southern Texas and New Mexico south to Peru. In the Caribbean it occurs in the Greater Antilles. The Antillean form has been proposed as a separate species, the Fulvous Swallow *(Petrochelidon fulva)*, distinct from the Cave Swallow *(Petrochelidon pelodoma)* of the southwestern USA and Mexico.

Black Swift
Cypseloides niger
Vencejo Negro

An all-black bird that flies to great heights in search of insects. It has narrow, pointed wings, and a long, slightly forked tail. Length: 18 cm.; weight: 36 g. Although the swift catches insects like a swallow, and often flocks with swallows, it is closely related to hummingbirds---an example of convergent evolution. It has elaborate, aerial courtship rituals, and will copulate in the air. The nest is made of moss, ferns and rootlets, bound with mud, and is placed on a narrow ledge on a cliff, often near a waterfall. An uncommon, local species. Puerto Rican swifts may winter in South America, but their winter ground is still a mystery as is much of their biology. Regular over El Yunque and Maricao State Forest.

Bicknell's Thrush
Catharus bicknelli
Zorzal de Bicknell

A rare thrush, gray above with rufous-tinged wing feathers and tail. The underparts are white with bold black breast spots. Length: 16-17 cm.; weight: 26-30 g. A secretive bird of dense understory in high mountain forests, the total population is probably only 50,000 birds. Although most are thought to winter in Hispaniola, this species may be more common in the western mountains of Puerto Rico than currently suspected. Breeds in eastern Canada and New England.

Red-legged Thrush
Turdus plumbeus
Zorzal de Patas Coloradas
Zorzal de Patas Rojas

IDENTIFICATION: A gray bird with black and white throat streaks; and red legs, bill and eye ring. Length: 25-28 cm.; weight: 75 g.
HABITAT: Forests, coffee plantations, and wooded gardens.
HABITS: Walks upright on the forest floor or on shaded roadsides in search of food. The Red-legged Thrush is especially active at dawn and dusk when it sings or calls high in a tree. But the rest of the day it is less obvious in denser vegetation, or offers just a fleeting glimpse as it flies across a road or forest clearing. Its food is mostly fruits, but a third of its diet is animal matter: insects (caterpillars, beetles, ants, crickets, wasps), plus occasional snails, frogs, lizards and birds' eggs. The thrush often flips over leaves on the forest floor to discover insects. It feeds on fruits either while perched or sometimes while hovering. The song at dawn is a prolonged series of repeated notes, with a pause between each note. The call notes include a harsh "*wek-wek.*" It places its nest of leaves and grasses on a tree limb, and lays 3-4 light green or white eggs. It can be attracted to feeders, which it will defend against grackles and doves.

STATUS AND CONSERVATION: A common permanent resident.
RANGE: Occurs in the Bahamas and the Greater Antilles (Cuba, Hispaniola, and Puerto Rico). An isolated race also occurs on Dominica, 300 miles southeast of Puerto Rico.

Northern Mockingbird   *Mimus polyglottos*   **Ruiseñor**

IDENTIFICATION: A long-tailed, flamboyant bird; gray above and white below, with a white wing patch. Length: 23-28 cm.; weight: 43-50 g.

HABITAT: Farms, open country and towns.

HABITS: Often seen throughout the day on wires and other exposed perches, where it guards its territory---aggressively chasing cats, kingbirds, hawks and other mockingbirds. Its white wing and tail patches flash dramatically as it chases an intruder. The song is a rambling, musical series of repeated phrases. The mockingbird often imitates other birds, as well as cats, cars, motors, and other odd noises in its environment. Birds that it likes to imitate include the Gray Kingbird, Red-legged Thrush and Black-whiskered Vireo. One mockingbird in North America was recorded as singing 194 different phrases. Its Latin name, *polyglottos*, refers to this varied song. Both sexes will sing, but unmated males may sing persistently at night---especially under bright moonlight or street lights---much to the distress of humans trying to sleep. The mockingbird sings from exposed perches, including antennae, and sometimes sings while leaping briefly into the air---like a rock star in concert. Its imitations can sometimes confuse human listeners. Once the author crashed into a brush-filled ditch to rescue an injured puppy, only to find that the "puppy" was a mockingbird! This species has several harsh calls including a *"chak"* note given at any time of year. Both males and females of neighboring pairs will patrol territorial lines to clearly mark their boundary. It has a varied diet---mostly berries and seeds---but 1/3 of the diet consists of spiders and insects, especially caterpillars, moths, grasshoppers, crickets and beetles, with a few ants and flies for variety. It builds a cup nest in a bush; the nest contains 3-4 spotted, green eggs. The female does most of the incubating while the male will later help in caring for the young. The mockingbird can be attracted to backyard bird feeders.

STATUS AND CONSERVATION: A very adaptable and common bird in the lowlands of Puerto Rico, especially on the south coast. Mockingbirds in Puerto Rico were commonly kept as pets for their song, and sold for $10-15 apiece in the early 20th Century. They were kept in a simple cage made of a gourd, with a string mesh on one side. Some people still keep them illegally as pets.

RANGE: Occurs from southeastern Canada to southern Mexico; and in the Caribbean from the Bahamas east to the Virgin Islands.

Pearly-eyed Thrasher *Margarops fuscatus* **Zorzal Pardo**

IDENTIFICATION: A long-tailed bird, related to the Northern Mockingbird. The upper parts are brown, and underparts are white, streaked with brown. The light-colored eye contrasts with the brown head. In flight the white tail markings often are striking. Length: 28-30 cm.; weight: 95-101 g.

HABITAT: Bushes and trees in gardens, mountain forests, coffee plantations.

HABITS: A curious, aggressive opportunist that feeds mostly on large insects, such as crickets, beetles, and walking sticks. It also eats fruits and berries, and sometimes lizards, frogs, small crabs, and other birds' eggs and nestlings. The song is a series of two or three melodic phrases separated by a pause, described as *"wheur, tel leur, tsee."* It makes a loud, whining alarm note, and also has a variety of single call notes, sometimes quite faint. It makes its stick nest in a tree cavity and lays 2-4 blue eggs.

STATUS AND CONSERVATION: A common species, even in city gardens, but it has a patchy distribution. The Pearly-eyed Thrasher was rare on the main island of Puerto Rico at the beginning of the 20th Century, but has now become common. It is possible that the species only expanded its range into Puerto Rico in recent centuries. The thrasher attacks nestlings of other species, possibly to reduce food competition or discourage nesting in scarce nest cavities. In one study at Roosevelt Roads, 43% of White-Crowned Pigeon nests experienced thrasher predation. The thrasher's habit of preying on other birds' eggs and chicks makes it a local threat to some species, such as the endangered Puerto Rican Parrot.

RANGE: Found in the Bahamas, Puerto Rico and most of the eastern Caribbean.

Northern Parula   *Parula americana*   **Reinita Pechidorada**

IDENTIFICATION: A small warbler with bluish upper parts, a green back, white wing bars, and a yellow throat and breast. The male has an orange breast band. Length: 11-12 cm.; weight: 5.5-11.2 g.

HABITAT: Multiple forest types: primary forest, mangroves, coffee plantations, gardens, coastal scrub, and scrubby cattle pastures. See also the endemic Adelaide's Warbler (page 23).

HABITS: The Parula feeds by gleaning its prey off leaves and branches, but will also hover, or hawk insects in mid-air. In winter, the Parula often feeds alone, but may join mixed flocks with other species. It sometimes defends a small, core feeding territory against other Parulas, Cape May Warblers and Prairie Warblers. The winter diet is mostly insects such as beetles, caterpillars, lantern flies, bugs, and some wasps. Spiders make up a large part of the diet as well. Birds that breed in eastern North America are thought to winter in the Caribbean, while birds that breed in central North America are more likely to winter in Central America. Some Parulas arrive in Puerto Rico as early as August, and begin to leave the Caribbean for the spring migration north as early as February, with most birds having departed by May.

STATUS AND CONSERVATION: A common migrant. The breeding range has contracted due to forest fragmentation and the impact of air pollution on tree lichens needed for nest building.

RANGE: Breeds from southeastern Canada and the Great Lakes region to coastal Texas and central Florida. Winters in the Caribbean and less commonly Central America.

Prothonotary Warbler
Protonotaria citrea
Reinita Anaranjada

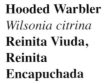

A bright yellow warbler with a green back and blue-gray wings and tail. Length: 14 cm.; weight: 14-16 g. An uncommon winter resident in mangroves and coastal areas in Puerto Rico, it breeds in swamps of the eastern USA. Breeding populations have declined (-1.5% per year in the period 1966-1995), possibly due to wetlands destruction and cowbird nest parasitism.

Hooded Warbler
Wilsonia citrina
Reinita Viuda, Reinita Encapuchada

A bright yellow face surrounded by a black hood identify this warbler. A white flash is visible in the tail as it flies. Females do not have complete hoods. Length: 13.3 cm.; weight: 11 g. Breeds in the eastern USA, and winters primarily from lowland Mexico south to Panamá. Uncommon in forests and coastal swamps. More common in the mountains of Puerto Rico than is generally recognized.

Yellow Warbler
Dendroica petechia
Canario de Mangle

IDENTIFICATION: A bright yellow bird with a green-tinged back. The male has orange streaking on the breast and sometimes the crown. Length: 12-13 cm.; weight: 9-11 g. See also photo on p. 10.
HABITAT: Mangroves, coastal dry forests, and large shrubs near water, in marshes, and along the coast and lowland rivers.

HABITS: Feeds on insects and spiders by plucking them off leaves or bark, and occasionally hovering. In mangroves, it often forages from the roots above the water and sometimes on near-by mud. In Puerto Rico, beetles, crickets, flies, cicadas, caterpillars, dragonflies, and earwigs have been documented in its diet. The song is an accelerating series of sweet notes, often with a slurred ending. The female builds a nest of grasses and bark and incubates the 2-3 eggs for 11-12 days. Both sexes feed the young chicks, which fledge 9-12 days after hatching. Migrants breeding in North America have larger clutches of 4-5 eggs.
STATUS AND CONSERVATION: A common, permanent resident. Some Yellow Warblers that breed in North America winter in Puerto Rico. Frequently parasitized by cowbirds.
RANGE: Breeds from northern Alaska and Quebec south to Venezuela. Typical in mangroves, such as at Cabo Rojo and Boquerón Nature Reserve. Taxonomists have lumped them into three subspecies complexes: the *aestiva* group that nests in North America, the Golden Warbler (*petechia* group) of the Caribbean which tends to be darker and greener, and the Mangrove Warbler (*erithachorides* group) of Central America that often has a chestnut head.

Magnolia Warbler
Dendroica magnolia
Reinita Manchada

The male has bright blue and black upperparts; white markings around the eye; and dramatic black streaks on a yellow breast. In winter these colors are more sub-dued (see photo at right). Length: 11-13 cm.; weight: 8-10 g. Breeds in North America, but is irruptive, i.e. in most winters the Magnolia Warbler is rare in Puerto Rico, but in other years it is much more common.

Black-throated Blue Warbler
Dendroica caerulescens
Reinita Azul

IDENTIFICATION: The male is deep blue above, with a black face, throat, and sides. The female is dull olive above, without the black undersides (photo at right). Both sexes have a distinctive, white wing-patch. The male and female look so different that some early scientists considered them distinct species. Length: 12-13 cm.; weight: 10 g.
HABITAT: Wet, dry and elfin forests, gardens, and shade-grown coffee plantations.
HABITS: Feeds on insects and spiders by hovering, or flying past a leaf and plucking off the prey. Also feeds on fruits, such as *Miconia*. Males prefer taller trees at low to middle altitudes, while females are more common in lower vegetation at high altitudes. Both sexes maintain a winter territory of about 1/4 hectare, and often return to the same site in successive winters.
STATUS AND CONSERVATION: One of the commonest winter warblers in Puerto Rican forests, this species has benefited from the recovery of forests on its breeding grounds.
RANGE: Breeds in deciduous forests of much of eastern North America. Almost all individuals of this species winter in the Greater Antilles. A regular place to find this species is in the forest above the El Portal visitor center in El Yunque.

Cape May Warbler
Dendroica tigrina
Reinita Tigre

A bright yellow warbler with dark streaks on the breast, and yellow rump and neck patches. The breeding male also has chestnut cheek patches. Females and immatures are duller olive green. Length: 12 cm.; weight: 9-11 g. Forages for insects and spiders along edges of moist forest, and in dry scrub forest, coffee plantations, mangroves, and gardens. It is the only warbler with a tubular tongue, adapted for sipping nectar. On the breeding grounds in North America, it specializes on Spruce Budworms (*Choristoneura fumiferana*), and its population increases locally during the cyclical outbreaks of this caterpillar. A common but irregular winter resident. Almost all Cape May Warblers winter in the Greater Antilles. Regular at Cabo Rojo National Wildlife Refuge.

Prairie Warbler
Dendroica discolor
Reinita Galana

IDENTIFICATION: A bright yellow warbler with an olive back, black streaking on the sides, and a distinctive black and yellow facial pattern. Length: 11 cm.; weight: 6.4-8.8 g.
HABITAT: Edges of moist or dry forest, abandoned fields with scattered shrubs, mangroves, coffee plantations, and gardens.
HABITS: This species bobs its tail frequently, as it forages in trees and shrubs. It gleans insects off leaves, and in winter also feeds on fruit and nectar. The Prairie Warbler is often seen alone, but sometimes joins mixed-species flocks. The call is a sharp "*tchick*" note. Just before migration, many individuals sing at dawn or dusk. The song is a high-pitched series of buzzy notes, rising in pitch.
STATUS AND CONSERVATION: A common winter resident. On the breeding grounds in the eastern USA, the Prairie Warbler increased as agricultural fields were abandoned in the early and mid-20th Century. But as these same areas matured into forest too dense for this species, the Prairie Warbler declined by over 50% in the last three decades. Cowbird nest parasitism is also a problem.
RANGE: Breeds from southern Ontario through the eastern USA. Winters from Florida south through the Caribbean, rarely wintering in Central America. Regular at Guánica State Forest.

Yellow-rumped Warbler
Dendroica coronata
Reinita Coronada

A large warbler with a yellow rump and sides, and white corners to the tail. Length: 13-14 cm.; weight: 12-13 g. Breeds in forests from Alaska east to Laborador and West Virginia. In most winters it is rare, but in some years larger numbers reach Puerto Rico. In winter it forages for berries and insects in shrubby fields, coastal areas, gardens, and edges of dry and moist forests. Besides gleaning insects, it will often hawk them in the air.

Palm Warbler
Dendroica palmarum
Reinita Palmera

The Palm Warbler has a streaked breast and yellow undertail coverts (the feathers under the base of the tail). In breeding plumage, the male has a bright rusty cap and yellow undersides streaked with rufous. Length: 12-14 cm.; weight: 10-12 g. Winters in mangroves, dry forest and brushy areas near coastal swamps. More than any other warbler, it has the habit of pumping its tail up and down as it walks on the ground, or hops in low bushes to feed on insects and spiders. It also adds nectar to its diet on the winter grounds, and will protect a favorite flowering plant from other birds. As with other warblers, this species migrates at night. A North American breeder, this species is uncommon and irregular in winter.

Black-and-white Warbler
Mniotilta varia
Reinita Trepadora

IDENTIFICATION: The male has a bold pattern of black and white stripes and streaks on the back, undersides and head, and has two white wing bars. The female lacks the male's black cheek and throat patches and has duller black streaking below. The long bill is slightly curved, which aids in extracting insects from bark crevices. Similarly the legs and toes are adapted to creeping on tree bark. Length: 13 cm.; weight: 10 g. See also the similar, endemic Elfin-woods Warbler on page 24.

HABITAT: Mangroves, shade coffee plantations, gardens and forests at all elevations.

HABITS: The Black-and-white Warbler has a unique feeding pattern. It flies to the base of a tree trunk and then works its way carefully up the trunk and larger limbs, pausing occasionally to probe crevices in the tree's bark for insects and spiders. It also gleans caterpillars, ants, flies and other insects in mid-levels of the forest among bromeliads and leaves. It

frequently travels in mixed-species flocks, and individuals often return to the same winter area each year. The common song is a high-pitched series of rapidly rising and falling notes, given rarely in winter in Puerto Rico.

STATUS AND CONSERVATION: A common winter visitor.

RANGE: Breeds in woodlands of eastern North America west to central Canada. It winters from Florida and southern Texas, south to the northern Andes and throughout the West Indies. It is common in the forests of El Yunque and many other public forests.

Blackpoll Warbler
Dendroica striata
Reinita Rayada

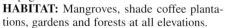

In breeding plumage, the male is black and white, with white cheek patches and yellow legs and feet. The non-breeding plumage is dull gray-brown with two white wing bars. Length: 13-14 cm.; weight: 12-13 g. Breeds in boreal forests from Alaska to New England. In fall it flies east across North America to Canada's Maritime Provinces and then flies over open ocean to winter grounds in northern South America. This migration sometimes takes three days nonstop over water.

American Redstart   *Setophaga ruticilla*   **Candelita**

IDENTIFICATION: The male is black with bold orange patches on the wings, sides, and tail. The more commonly seen female and immature birds are gray above and white below, and the orange patches are replaced by yellow. Length: 13 cm.; weight: 7-8 g.

HABITAT: Winters in forests, mangroves, shade coffee plantations, and urban gardens.

HABITS: Constantly flicks its tail and wings open and closed, as it forages for insects (beetles, flies, lantern flies, and small wasps), spiders, and occasionally fruits. It often snatches insects in mid-air or hovers to pick insects off leaves. It has a relatively wide base to the bill, and stiff bristles around its mouth, like a flycatcher. These features aid in catching insects in mid-air. The redstart is more likely to flycatch for food in Puerto Rico and elsewhere in winter, than on its breeding grounds. In winter the redstart defends a feeding territory, and often returns to the same territory each winter. It joins mixed-species flocks as they pass through its territory. Females in Puerto Rico are somewhat more likely to inhabit dry forest, in part because older males aggressively exclude others of their species from prime winter feeding grounds. Breeds in young deciduous forests or forest clearings in North America.

STATUS AND CONSERVATION: A common winter visitor. It is threatened on its breeding grounds by cowbird nest parasitism, deforestation, aging of eastern forests, and forest fragmentation. Population declines have been recorded in some regions of North America.

RANGE: Breeds in open woodlands in much of the eastern USA and southern Canada, west to Oregon and the Yukon Territory. It winters from southern Florida and lowland Mexico south, through Central America and the Caribbean, to northern Peru and Brazil.

Yellow-throated Warbler
Dendroica dominica
Reinita de Garganta Amarilla

A gray-backed warbler with a yellow throat, black streaks on white sides, and a distinctive black-and-white face pattern. Length: 13-16 cm.; weight: 10-11 g. Breeds in North America. Uncommon in winter in palms, mangroves, and coastal scrub. It uses its relatively long bill to probe crevices and leaf clusters for insects that are out of reach for many other warblers.

Louisiana Waterthrush
Seiurus motacilla
Pizpita de Río

IDENTIFICATION: An active, ground-feeding warbler with a brown back, streaked undersides, a wide, white eye line, and pink legs. Its bill is larger than in the Northern Waterthrush. Length: 15 cm.; weight: 16 g.
HABITAT: Forested streams.
HABITS: Forages along streamsides and wet forest roads. Constantly rocks on its legs, bobbing its lower body and tail up and down. It gleans insects from the edge of the water, just below the water's surface, or from stream side vegetation. It will also flip over submerged leaves to discover food, and rarely catches airborne insects by hovering or hawking. Although most food in Puerto Rico is documented to be insects (such as flies, beetles, dragonflies), it also eats small snails, scorpions, and frogs. Each bird defends a narrow, streamside territory 100-300 meters long in winter. It frequently gives a loud "*chink*" note.
STATUS AND CONSERVATION: A common, winter resident.
RANGE: Breeds along streams in eastern North America. Regular along streams and wet forest roads in El Yunque.

Northern Waterthrush
Seiurus noveboracensis
Pizpita de Mangle

IDENTIFICATION: Similar to the Louisiana Waterthrush, but smaller, with a smaller bill, a narrower and more buffy eye line, more streaking on the throat, and browner legs. Length: 15 cm. Average weight in winter is 15-16 g. As with other long distance migrants, it puts on lots of fat before its southbound migration, increasing its body weight to 24 g.
HABITAT: Mangrove swamps.

HABITS: The Northern Waterthrush bobs its tail and lower body as it hops along fallen tree trunks and mangrove roots and in shallow water and mudflats below the trees. It forages for insects, spiders, and occasionally tiny crabs. Each bird maintains a winter territory of about 1/2 hectare. Frequently gives a sharper, more metallic call note than the Louisiana Waterthrush's.
STATUS AND CONSERVATION: A common, winter resident. Although the North American breeding range is still extensive, mangroves in its winter range have been extensively cut. About half the original mangrove forest of Puerto Rico has been cut down.
RANGE: Breeds in boreal forest swamps in northern North America. Winters throughout the Caribbean and Central America to Brazil. Regular at Parque Central in San Juan.

Ovenbird
Seiurus aurocapilla
Pizpita Dorada

IDENTIFICATION: An olive-backed warbler with bold, black streaks on the breast and an orange central stripe on the crown. Length: 15 cm.; weight: 19-21 g.
HABITAT: This species is a "generalist" among the migrant warblers. It is found at ground level in mangroves, wetlands, shade coffee, and other forests, especially with a well-developed shrub layer.
HABITS: The Ovenbird is quite inconspicuous as it walks on the forest floor, searching the leaf litter and occasionally small shrubs for insects, spiders, snails, and other invertebrates. As it inspects fallen tree trunks and flicks over dead leaves, it pumps its tail and sometimes holds it cocked upwards. It often returns to the same winter feeding area each year. Birds that winter in the Caribbean are thought to breed east of the Appalachian Mountains.
STATUS AND CONSERVATION: A common, but quiet and secretive forest species in winter. Its population has declined because of fragmentation of breeding areas in North American forests. Forest fragmentation allows predators and cowbirds easier access to forest birds' nests. In some places, Brown-headed Cowbirds lay eggs in more than half of all Ovenbird nests, which reduces the nest success of the host bird. Many Ovenbirds also die in collisions with communications towers and buildings during night-time migration.
RANGE: Breeds in deciduous forests of southern Canada and the eastern and central USA. It winters through most of Mexico and Central America to northern Venezuela, and from southern Florida through the Bahamas, the Greater Antilles and the Virgin Islands. Regular at Guánica State Forest.

Common Yellowthroat
Geothlypis trichas
Reinita Pica Tierra

IDENTIFICATION: A bright yellow throat, black face mask bordered with white, and an olive brown back distinguish the male. The female lacks the mask, but has a thin, white eye ring. Length: 11-13 cm.; weight: 9-10 g.
HABITAT: Marshes, canal edges, mangrove borders, dry forest, brushy areas, and moist fields with tall grass.
HABITS: Spends much of the winter hidden in dense thickets, but will hop into the open to investigate an intruder. Readily responds to humans' squeaking or "pishing" noises. It often cocks its tail as it quickly forages for insects, spiders and some seeds. Has a distinctive, hoarse "*djip*" call note. The song on the breeding grounds is a monotonous "*witchity-witchity-witchity.*" The female builds a bulky nest, hidden in brush or tall marsh vegetation. She does all the incubating of the 3-5 eggs for about 12 days. Both parents feed the young, which leave the nest 10 days after hatching.
STATUS AND CONSERVATION: A common winter resident. It has increased with the abandoning of farms in the breeding range, but is commonly parasitized by cowbirds.
RANGE: Breeds from southern Canada to northern Mexico. It winters from the southern USA through Central America and the Greater Antilles. Regular at the Humacao Nature Reserve.

Bananaquit
Coereba flaveola
Reinita

IDENTIFICATION: The only Puerto Rican land bird with a short, strongly curved bill, the Bananaquit is black above, with a dark gray throat, and a bright yellow belly. It has a white eye stripe and wing patch. Length: 10-12 cm.; weight: 9-10 g.
HABITAT: Occurs wherever there are trees, bushes or flowers.
HABITS: The Bananaquit is bold, acrobatic, and noisy. It is in constant motion, flitting its wings as it feeds at all elevations in the forest on flower nectar, fruits, insects and spiders. It can be attracted to gardens and patios by sugar water feeders, or may just invite itself to the family sugar bowl. It sometimes "robs" nectar by piercing the base of a flower. In forested areas, the Bananaquit often joins tanagers and migrant warblers in mixed-species foraging flocks. The variable song has been described as an accelerating, insect-like trill: "*zee-e-e-e swees se tee.*" It sings throughout the day. It also makes a variety of drawn out, buzzy notes. The male defends a territory, but usually tolerates females and juveniles in the territory. Both sexes build the nest, which is a unique ball of grasses, moss,

fine sticks, and other vegetation—and non-vegetative matter—with an entrance hole underneath or on the side, containing 2-3 brown-spotted eggs. May nest several times in one year. The Bananaquit often builds separate nests as safe, night time roosts, and takes nest material from an old nest to build a new one a short distance away.
STATUS AND CONSERVATION: The most abundant bird in Puerto Rico. In some forest areas, 2/3 of all birds are Bananaquits. Population density of this species has been estimated at up to 10 birds per hectare in some locations.
RANGE: Occurs throughout the Caribbean islands, except Cuba. It also occurs on the mainland from Mexico, south to Peru, Paraguay, northeastern Argentina, and southern Brazil.

Antillean Euphonia
Euphonia musica
Jilguero, Canario del País

IDENTIFICATION: The male has a bright yellow rump and undersides, an orange forehead, a bright blue crown, and a blue-black back, tail, wings and cheeks. The female is dull olive green, with a lighter blue cap than the male's. Length: 10-12 cm.; weight: 13-16 g.

HABITAT: Mountain forests, shade coffee plantations, and lowland dry scrub forests.

HABITS: Travels in small flocks in search of its favorite food: the fruits of mistletoe (*Phoradendron* sp.). Several birds will forage in a single clump of mistletoe and then travel some distance in an undulating flight, to another mistletoe clump. The birds defecate mistletoe seeds that are very sticky and cling to tree branches, thus facilitating the dispersal of the parasitic mistletoe plant to different trees. The call is a single or double, tinkling note that sounds like a tiny bell, "*chit-it.*" Euphonias make a domed nest with an entrance on the side, and lay 3-4 white eggs with reddish brown speckling at the large end.

STATUS AND CONSERVATION: An uncommon, localized forest species. The Euphonia was marketed as a popular cage bird in Puerto Rico because of its beautiful plumage and song. It sold for 5 to 10 cents apiece in markets at the beginning of the 20th Century. However, all native birds in Puerto Rico are now protected by law, and it is illegal to keep any native species as a pet. After severe hurricanes, such as Hurricane Georges in 1998, Euphonias abandon many forests, since the fruits that they depend on are destroyed by high winds or treefall. The Antillean Euphonia appeared on a 32-cent US postage stamp (1998 Tropical Bird stamp series # 445915).

RANGE: Occurs on Hispaniola, Puerto Rico and most of the islands in the eastern Caribbean. Regular near Ciales and on the forested trail around Parador Hacienda Juanita in Marico.

Rose-breasted Grosbeak
Pheucticus lucovicianus
Picogrueso Pechirrojo

A black and white finch with a red breast, white wing bars and a large, pale bill. Females are brown above and white below with a prominent eye line. Length: 19 cm.; weight: 42 g. Rare visitor to Puerto Rico. It breeds in deciduous forests of eastern North America. Unlike most bird species, the male will sometimes sing from the nest.

Scarlet Tanager
Piranga olivacea
Cardenal, Escarlatina

In breeding plumage, the male is bright red with black wings and tail. The female and non-breeding male are green or olive green, with darker wings and tail. Length: 18 cm.; weight: 28 g. Breeds in deciduous forests of eastern North America; winters in the northern Andes. Rare migrant in coastal Puerto Rico. See also the endemic Puerto Rican Spindalis and Puerto Rican Tanager on pages 25-26.

Yellow-faced Grassquit
Tiaris olivaceus
Gorrión Barba Amarilla

IDENTIFICATION: A small, olive-green finch with a black bib, and a yellow throat and eyeline. The female lacks the black bib and has fainter yellow head markings. Length: 11-12 cm.; weight: 7-9 g.
HABITAT: Open, brushy fields, marshy areas, and roadsides with tall grass.
HABITS: Travels in flocks and feeds on small seeds close to the ground or from tall grasses. It will also eat some fruits, small insects and spiders. Sometimes flies to the top of a grass stalk and rides it to the ground to get at the seeds. The song is a weak, prolonged, rattly trill, repeated on several pitches. The male sings hidden in tall grass, or visible from the top of a grass stalk or on a more conspicuous bush, post, fence or wire. Its nest is a low, globular grass structure with an entrance on the side, and contains 3-4 bluish or greenish-white eggs with brown spots.
STATUS AND CONSERVATION: A common species in open country, but has narrower habitat preferences than the Black-faced Grassquit. It may eventually experience some reduction in population as urban development replaces open fields.
RANGE: Occurs throughout the Greater Antilles and from Mexico to Venezuela.

Black-faced Grassquit
Tiaris bicolor
Gorrión Negro

IDENTIFICATION: A small finch with a dark, olive-green back, and black head and undersides. The female is dull olive but without the faint yellow head markings of the Yellow-faced Grassquit. Length: 11-12 cm.; weight: 9-10 g. See also the endemic Puerto Rican Bullfinch on page 27.
HABITAT: Open, brushy fields, gardens, open woodlands and forest clearings.
HABITS: Travels in pairs or flocks feeding close to the ground or exploring tree limbs. It feeds mostly on small seeds, plus insects and spiders. Readily attracted to bird-seed feeders, and can become relatively tame. Breeds throughout the year. Males sing all day in breeding season with a weak song: a two or three note, buzzy trill, somewhat like a Bananaquit's, but lower pitched. The male displays by calling, and fanning his tail and short wings simultaneously. He performs a courtship flight at slow speed, with trembling wings.
STATUS AND CONSERVATION: A common, adaptable species.
RANGE: Colombia and Venezuela; the Caribbean islands, except Cuba and the Caymans.

115

Saffron Finch
Sicalis flaveola
Pinzón Azafrán

A canary-like, yellow finch with an orange wash to the crown. Length: 14 cm. This species is common in parks, golf course edges, and gardens in Puerto Rico. The song is a musical series of chips. It builds its nest in holes in buildings or trees, or clumps of palm leaves. Introduced from South America where it is found from Colombia and the Guianas south to northwestern Peru and northern Argentina. A regular location to find this species is on the lawns at the government office buildings at San Juan's Isla Grande airport.

Grasshopper Sparrow
Ammodramus savannarum
Gorrión Chicharra

IDENTIFICATION: A small, brown bird with a large, flat head, short tail, and a small orange spot in front of the eye. The crown has a buffy white stripe in the center. Length: 11-12 cm.; weight: 15-19 g. The Puerto Rican subspecies, *Ammodromus savannarum borinquensis*, is smaller and has a brighter central crown stripe than many other subspecies.

HABITAT: Weedy fields and pastures with tall grass and isolated bushes.

HABITS: Feeds on insects and seeds on the ground or in low grasses and shrubs. In one study of stomach contents, 1/3 of the diet in Puerto Rico was seeds, and the remainder consisted of insects: beetles, crickets, ants, bugs, and caterpillars. The male has two very different songs: an insect-like, accelerating trill; also a high-pitched jumble of notes. This species can be hard to see, since it spends much of its time foraging on the ground below tall grass. The exception is during the breeding season when the male sings from the top of a grass stalk or shrub to advertise his territory. He sometimes displays by singing during a slow, fluttery flight over his territory. The female builds a well-hidden nest on the ground under an arch of grasses. She incubates 3-5 eggs for 11-12 days. Both sexes feed the young. This species shifts breeding sites, as vegetation conditions change.

STATUS AND CONSERVATION: A common, permanent resident in grasslands in Puerto Rico. This species is often overlooked because of its weak song, and drab plumage. The clearing of forests in the 19th Century created new habitat for this species, but the recent expansion of urban areas has reduced grassland habitat. Mongooses are a threat to this, as well as other ground-nesting birds.

RANGE: Breeds from southern Canada to northern Mexico, plus Jamaica, Hispaniola and Puerto Rico. Regular in short grass fields near Caño Tiburones Nature Reserve.

Greater Antillean Grackle
Quiscalus niger
Mozambique, Chango

IDENTIFICATION: An iridescent black bird with a long, narrow bill, long tail, and bright yellow eyes. The female is smaller and less iridescent than the male. Juvenile birds have brown eyes. Some rare individuals have varying amounts of white body feathers. Length: 25-30 cm.; weight: males 87 g., females 65 g.

HABITAT: Farms, open country and towns; avoids deep forest.

HABITS: Boldly walks on the ground looking for food in fields, gardens, stream banks, and even parking lots and inside open-air restaurants. The grackle often holds its outer tail feathers higher than the central tail feathers. This results in a "V"-shaped appearance to the tail when viewed from in front or behind. It eats fruits, nectar, seeds, ticks, frogs, lizards, snails, and discarded human food including bread, French fries, beans, and meat scraps. But most of the diet consists of insects, such as crickets, grasshoppers, roaches, weevils, and caterpillars. It sometimes raids other birds' nests. It makes a variety of whistles and clucking call notes, e.g., a thin high "*tee tee tee.*" It also has a common call note, "*chuck.*" When displaying on the ground or along a palm leaf, it throws its

head back and points its bill to the sky. It also has a "ruff out" display (see top photo) in which it fluffs its feathers and sings, while spreading its wings and tail. The grackle roosts in large noisy flocks at night in protected trees, such as in town plazas. It nests in loose colonies in the tops of trees, palms, or even electrical power substations. The grackle makes a cup-shaped nest of grasses and sticks combined with artificial materials such as paper, plastic, wire, straws, and mop strings. She lays 3-5 bluish or olive eggs with red or black speckles. The young fledge about 23 days after hatching. This species is easily attracted to bird feeders.

STATUS AND CONSERVATION: A common bird of towns and open country, especially in lowland Puerto Rico. Grackle chicks in nests that have been parasitized by Shiny Cowbirds have a lower growth rate than grackle chicks in nests without cowbird chicks. But the female grackle will often eject cowbird eggs.

RANGE: As its name implies, the Greater Antillean Grackle occurs only in the Greater Antilles. There are seven subspecies of this bird. The endemic Puerto Rican subspecies (*Quiscalus niger brachypterus*) is larger than the subspecies on Hispaniola. Five related species occur elsewhere in the Americas.

Shiny Cowbird
Molothrus bonariensis
Tordo

IDENTIFICATION: The Shiny Cowbird has a stout, pointed bill. Males are a shiny purple-black color, while females are a dull, gray-brown. In flight the cowbird appears smaller and more slender than the Greater Antillean Grackle and has a narrower tail. Length: 18-20 cm.; weight: males 40 g., females 34 g.
HABITAT: Prefers open or brushy fields, often near livestock, but can be found in open forests, or gardens as well.
HABITS: As its name suggests, the Shiny Cowbird does feed near cattle, but can forage in any open field for grain, seeds and insects. The cowbird travels in flocks either with its own species or in the company of Greater Antillean Grackles or Yellow-shouldered Blackbirds (page 28). The male's song is a series of bubbly notes followed by a whistle. The bird fluffs up the feathers around its neck as it utters these notes and often sings while flying. The female has a brief, bubbly "chatter" call. Also makes a high-pitched, whistled contact call. The cowbird spends the night in a communal roost. It does not build a nest of its own, but parasitizes other birds' nests. Nest parasitism harms the host bird in a number of ways. Sometimes the female cowbird ejects the host's eggs. The nest's builder will sometimes abandon the nest if it recognizes the alien cowbird egg, or sometimes will build another nest layer on top of the original nest, thus killing both its own eggs and the cowbird's egg. Often the cowbird chick grows more rapidly than the chicks of the nest's builder, and deprives them of food resources. Throughout its range in the Americas, the Shiny Cowbird has been documented to parasitize the nests of over 201 species of other birds, including Yellow Warbler, Greater Antillean Oriole, and Black-whiskered Vireo.
STATUS AND CONSERVATION: Originally native to South America, during the 20th Century it expanded its range, taking advantage of habitat changes due to agriculture and cattle ranching. The cowbird was documented to breed in Puerto Rico about 1955. Its breeding behavior of parasitizing other birds' nests has reduced the nesting success of the endemic Puerto Rican Vireo and Yellow-shouldered Blackbird. A trapping program to remove cowbirds in southwestern Puerto Rico is a key strategy to keep the blackbird from becoming extinct on the main island of Puerto Rico.
RANGE: Breeds from southern Florida to Chile. It is now found throughout Puerto Rico, especially in agricultural areas.

Greater Antillean Oriole
(Puerto Rican Oriole)
Icterus dominicensis
Calandria

IDENTIFICATION: The adult is black, with a yellow wing patch, and yellow patches on the rump and on the underside at the base of the tail. Immature birds are olive green. Length: 20-22 cm.; weight: 37 g. See also the endemic Yellow-shouldered Blackbird on page 28.
HABITAT: Forests, including shade-grown coffee plantations, citrus orchards, mangroves, palm groves, gardens.

HABITS: Eats mostly insects in the forest canopy and mid-story, but also consumes fruits and juices of overripe oranges. Prey include earwigs, crickets, grasshoppers, roaches, cicadas, weevils, caterpillars, ants, wasps, spiders, scorpions, lizards and frogs. It has unusually strong muscles at the base of the skull that allow it to open its bill against resistance. Thus the oriole can pry open bromeliads, curled leaves, or bark—a technique known as "gaping." It methodically hops from one branch to the next, sometimes hanging upside down, to inspect likely locations for insects. The song is a series of high-pitched whistles, given mostly at dawn. Its fibrous, hanging nest is often placed in a palm tree. The female does most of the nest building, incubating its 3-4 brownish or bluish eggs, and feeding the nestlings. Young birds often flock with the parents for much of the following year.

STATUS AND CONSERVATION: Common; threatened by cowbird nest parasitism.
RANGE: Cuba, Hispaniola, Puerto Rico, and the Bahamas. Formerly called Black-cowled Oriole, it was split from Central American forms *(Icterus prosthemelas)*. The Puerto Rican race *(Icterus dominicensis portoricensis)* is blacker than other races and may be a distinct species.

Baltimore Oriole   *Icterus galbula*   Calandria Migratoria

The male has a black hood and upper back; the underparts and rump are orange, as are the outer feathers on the black tail. The female is duller orange below, with an olive-brown back, wings and tail. Both sexes have white wing bars. Length: 18-20 cm.; weight: 30-40 g. Open woodlands, dry forests, and gardens. Eats mostly spiders and insects, which it gleans from leaves. Also eats some snails, fruits and nectar. Nests in North America. A rare winter visitor to Puerto Rico,

but reported regularly from Hacienda Juanita and other spots in the southwest.

Troupial
Icterus icterus
Turpial

IDENTIFICATION: Bright yellow-orange, with a black back, tail, head and breast. The margin between the black breast and orange undersides is ragged. The wings are black, with a large white patch. At close range, the bright blue skin around the eye can be seen. Immature birds are more yellowish. Length: 25 cm.; weight: 72 g.

HABITAT: Dry deciduous forest, thorn scrub, open wooded country, palm groves, and suburban gardens.

HABITS: Often travels in pairs, or small family groups feeding on fruits of royal palm, sebucán (*Cephalocereus*), and other plants. In the breeding season it increases the proportion of protein in its diet by eating more insects, birds eggs and nestlings. Despite the fact that the Puerto Rican population may have originated from escaped or released caged birds, the Troupial is often wary of humans and typically does not allow close approach. The male and less commonly the female sing a whistled, variable, series of two or three note phrases. It builds its nest chiefly in April and May in a cactus, thorny bush or a tree, where it lays 2-4 spotted eggs. The female incubates the eggs for 15-16 days. Both parents feed the nestlings until they fledge about 21-23 days after hatching. In its native South America, the Troupial often takes over and uses abandoned nests of other bird species. Readily adapts to bird feeders.

STATUS AND CONSERVATION: The Troupial was probably introduced from South America, and has been reported in Puerto Rico since 1810. It is currently common, but was often captured for sale as a cage bird until the trade in wild birds was regulated. The Shiny Cowbird sometimes lays its eggs in Troupial nests.

RANGE: Native to the Amazon basin, and through most of northeastern Colombia and Venezuela (where it is the national bird). It has been introduced to a number of Caribbean islands. The Troupial is most common in southwestern Puerto Rico. A typical site to find this bird is on the trails at the eastern end of PR 333 in Guánica State Forest.

Red Siskin
Carduelis cucullata
Cardenalito

IDENTIFICATION: A rare, introduced finch, with dramatic differences between male and female plumages. The male has a black head, throat, tail and wings; with bright red back, undersides and wing patches. In contrast, the female is light gray with a salmon-colored rump, breast, and wing patches. Length: 10-11 cm.; weight: 10 g.
HABITAT: Dry, hilly grasslands with scattered trees and forest edges.
HABITS: Feeds in small flocks on seeds and fleshy fruits, often traveling large distances in a day. The song is described as a jumble of twitters and trills; the call is described as a raspy "*jut-jut.*" In its native habitat the female lays three to five eggs per clutch. Its habits are not well studied in Puerto Rico.

STATUS AND CONSERVATION: A native of northern South America and has been a popular cage bird since the 19th Century. In addition, aviculturists cross Red Siskins with the Island Canary (*Serinus canaria*) to breed in red-colored feathers and other traits. The wild population in Puerto Rico resulted from escaped or intentionally introduced captive birds. In South America the cage bird trade has decimated wild populations. It is quite rare and local throughout its range, with at most a few thousand birds in the wild. Proposed conservation measures there include protecting the few remaining breeding areas, and ultimately establishing a captive breeding and release program. Successful captive breeding efforts are under way in a number of countries, especially in Germany and the USA. In Puerto Rico, the Red Siskin is protected by regulations on the capture of introduced birds for the cage bird trade.

However, illegal trapping may eliminate this species from the island. There are no formal plans for habitat protection in Puerto Rico, but if the population survives here, it may offer a genetic reservoir for future efforts to conserve the species in its original range in South America.
RANGE: Native to foothills at 300-1,200 m elevation in northeastern Colombia and northern Venezuela; formerly in Trinidad. In Puerto Rico, Raffaele describes the Red Siskin as having occurred in the past in a triangle between the towns of Guayama, Coamo, and Aibonito; reports of this species from the Aibonito area in the last 10 years have not been confirmed by ornithologists.

House Sparrow
Passer domesticus
Gorrión Inglés

The male has a black bib, gray crown, a white wing bar, and chestnut eye patch, streaked brown back and wings. The female is a duller brown with light streaks on the back, and a buff eye line. Length: 15 cm.; weight: 27-30 g. Introduced from Europe to many cities of the Americas, where the beginnings of geographic races have started to evolve just over the last century. This species is found in urban areas throughout Puerto Rico, especially on the south coast where it was noted to be common in Ponce in the 1970s. It is thought to have been deliberately introduced or hitched a ride on cargo ships. It nests in holes in walls, light posts, or pipes, breeding throughout the year, but especially from March to September. Its song is a simple, cheery series of chip notes. Like many other species, the House Sparrow frequently takes dust baths to clean its skin and feathers of parasites and excess oils.

Indian Silverbill
Lonchura malabarica
Pinzón de Pico Plateado

Also called Warbling Silverbill, White-throated Munia or White-throated Silverbill, this small brown finch has a thick, dark gray or silver bill. Adults are light brown with darker wings, white rump, and a dark, pointed tail, while immatures (see right photo) are more uniformly dark brown. Length: 12 cm.; weight: 10-14 g. It lives in brushy fields and roadsides. Travels in small flocks and will often allow a close approach. Feeds on seeds. The call is a short, plaintive single or double note, often with a sharp inflection at the beginning. Nest is a spherical grass ball; 3-6 eggs. Locally common in coastal Puerto Rico, especially along the southwest coast. Introduced from India. Regular on the brushy slopes around the Cabo Rojo lighthouse and at La Parguera.

Nutmeg Mannikin
Lonchura punctulata
Pinzón Acanelado

Also called the Scaly-breasted Munia or Ricebird. The adult is brown above and on the throat, with a black scaling pattern on the white underside. Immatures are dull brown. Length: 11 cm.; weight: 12-15 g. The voice is a two-note call, higher pitched than the Bronze Mannikin's. Travels in flocks, sometimes with other finch species. Feeds on seeds. Wags tail. The female lays 4-6 white eggs in a round nest of grass hidden in a palm, shrub, or small tree. Native to Asia where it ranges from Indonesia west to Nepal, but most legal importations have been from India.

Bronze Mannikin
Lonchura cucullata
Diablito

The adult is dark gray above, white below, with an iri descent, dark hood and a thick gray bill. Immatures are dull brown. Length: 11 cm. The call is a low, "churring" note. Often perch side-by-side, in a row on a branch. This species is common in lowland gardens and weedlots where it feeds on small seeds. Introduced in the 18th or early 19th Centuries, presumably from the slavetraders' ports in Angola or São Tomé.

Orange Bishop
Euplectes franciscanus
Tejedor Rojo
Obispo Colorado

The breeding male is bright reddish-orange with a black belly and head. The female and non-breeding male are streaked with dark brown on the back, and have a yellow eye line, and a dark patch behind the eye. Length: 12 cm. Found in tall grass in lowlands, for example, in wet grassy fields near the Fajardo airport and at Laguna Cartagena National Wildlife Refuge. Importation records suggest that this and the related Yellow-crowned Bishop (*Euplectes afer*, Tejedor de Napoleón) derive from birds imported from Senegal. The bishops may become less common in Puerto Rico as rice cultivation and other agriculture declines. The Yellow-crowned Bishop is rare at Laguna Cartagena National Wildlife Refuge, Canóvanas, and Río Grande.

Tricolored Munia *Lonchura malacca* Monjita Tricolor

Formerly called the Chestnut Mannikin, the adults have a brown back; black hood and belly patch. Immatures are dull brown. Length: 11 cm.; weight: 10-15 g. Call is a nasal "*pwi-pwi*" like a tiny horn. Tends to travel in a constantly moving flock with others of its species, rather than mixing with other introduced finches. Roosts in nests at night. Feeds on seeds. As a flock takes off, the whirring of their wings is audible. The female lays 4-7 white eggs in a spherical nest in low vegetation. Introduced from Asia where it ranges from southern India to Sri Lanka, and is sometimes considered a pest in rice plantations. Most legal importations have been from India.

Orange-cheeked Waxbill
Estrilda melpoda
Veterano

A small brown finch with a large, orange cheek patch, and a bright red bill and rump. Length: 11 cm. Lives in grasslands and cultivated areas. It wags its tail from side to side as it forages for small seeds in tall grass. When not breeding, it travels in small flocks, sometimes with Bronze or Nutmeg Mannikins. The call is an abrupt "*jit.*" Song is a series of thin whistled notes. The nest is hidden in dense vegetation on the ground and contains 5-6 white eggs. Some nests are placed in odd locations such as between glass panes in an open window.   Common in the coastal lowlands of Puerto Rico.   Introduced to Puerto Rico and the Hawaiian Islands (Oahu). Native to Africa from Senegal and Angola, east to Chad and Zambia. This species is thought to have first been introduced via slave trading vessels from Angola in the early 19th Century. Regular places to find this species are the tall grass and marshy edges of the Humacao Nature Reserve and Laguna Cartagena National Wildlife Refuge.

Java Sparrow
Padda oryzivora
Gorrión de Java, Gorrión Arrocero

A large gray finch with a black head, distinctive white cheek patches and a thick, red bill. Length: 15 cm.; weight: 25 g. It inhabits grassy city parks and lowland suburban gardens. The Java Sparrow travels in small flocks feeding on seeds and small insects on lawns and in gardens. In Asia it is considered a pest in rice fields. The male sings a soft warble, and the call is a harsh "*clink*" note. Unlike most Puerto Rican birds, the Java Finch is stimulated to breed by decreasing, rather than increasing day length, so it breeds in fall and winter. It builds its dome-shaped nest in holes or under eaves of buildings. Clutch size is 3-8 eggs. This species is a popular, easy to raise cage bird that has escaped or been intentionally introduced in the 20th Century. Ironically, it is now more common in areas of the world where it has been introduced than it is in its native homeland. The Java Sparrow is established in the San Juan metropolitan area, and is one of the commoner bird species in Old San Juan. It is originally from Indonesia (Bali and Java) but has been introduced to Hawaii and many other tropical regions.

Pin-tailed Whydah
Vidua macroura
Viuda Colicinta

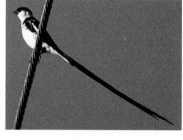

In breeding season, the male is black and white with a red bill, and a dramatic, 20 cm.-long, black tail streamer. The female and non-breeding male are brown above with a red bill, and black and white stripes on the face. Length: 12 cm., not counting tail. Forages in grasslands, sugar cane fields, and suburban lawns. In the breeding season the whydah follows flocks of other exotic finches. The male displays from exposed perches on branches and wires and circles above the female, performing a flight song: a prolonged twittering song; the call note is a sharp "*hwuit*." Feeds on seeds in fields; often flocks when not breeding. The female does not build a nest, but is a nest parasite, like the cowbird. She deposits her white eggs in the nests of other species, especially waxbills and other exotic finches. Regular but uncommon in the coastal lowlands of Puerto Rico. Introduced to Puerto Rico. Native to Africa, from Senegal and Congo, east to Eritrea, and south to South Africa, but most legal importations have been from Senegal. A regular place to find this species is the grassy fields and fence lines near La Parguera.

ORGANIZATIONS THAT SUPPORT BIRDING and CONSERVATION

Sociedad Ornitológica Puertorriqueña
PO Box 195166
San Juan. PR 00919-5166
http://www.avesdepuertorico.org/

Sociedad de Historia Natural de PR (Puerto Rico Natural History Association)
PO Box 361036
San Juan, PR 00936-1036
http://nhspr.org/

Puerto Rican Spindalis

Fideicomiso de Conservación
(Conservation Trust of Puerto Rico)
155 Calle Tetuan
Apartado Postal 9023554
San Juan, PR 00902
http://www.fideicomiso.org/

Guardianes de la Montaña
PO Box 1112
Ciales, PR 00638-1112

American Birding Association
PO Box 6599
Colorado Springs, CO 80934-6599
800-850-2473 or 719-578-1614
http://www.americanbirding.org/

American Bird Conservancy
1250 24th St., NW, Suite 400
Washington, DC 20037
202-778-9666
http://www.abcbirds.org

Partners In Flight coalition
http://www.PartnersInFlight.org

Laboratory of Ornithology
Cornell University
159 Sapsucker Woods Road
Ithaca, NY 14850
607-254-2473
http://birds.cornell.edu/

National Audubon Society
950 Third Avenue
New York, NY 10022
212-832-3200
http://www.audubon.org/

Departamento de Recursos Naturales
y Ambientales
Pda. 3½ Avenida Muñoz Rivera
Puerta de Tierra, Puerto Rico 00906-6600
Tel: 787-724-8774
http://www.gobierno.pr/drna

Society for the Conservation and Study of
Caribbean Birds
c/o Rosemarie Gnam, PhD
13 East Rosemont Ave.
Alexandria, VA 22301
703-739-9803
http://www.nmnh.si.edu/BIRDNET/SCSCB/index.html

Puerto Rican Tody

SOURCES OF INFORMATION

• Biaggi, V. 1997. Las aves de Puerto Rico. 4th Ed. Univ. de PR Press, Río Piedras. Natural history and folklore, but older taxonomy. Bibliography of pre-1982 publications.

• Camacho Rodríguez, M., J. Chabert Llompart, and M. López Flores. 1999. Guía para la identificación de las aves exóticas establecidas en Puerto Rico. Depto. de Recursos Naturales y Ambientales, San Juan, PR.

• Collar, N. J., L. P. Gonzaga, N. Krabbe, A. Madroño Nieto, L. G. Naranjo, T. A. Parker III, and D. G. Wege. 1992: Threatened birds of the Americas: the ICBP/IUCN Red data Book, 3rd Ed., part 2. Smithsonian Inst. Press. Detailed chapters on several of the rarer species.

• del Hoyo, J., A. Elliott, and J. Sargatal, eds. Handbook of Birds of the World. Lynx Edicions, Barcelona. Detailed species descriptions and family summaries; excellent color plates. 11 volumes available so far through 2006. http://www.hbw.com

• Ehrlich, P.R., D.S. Dobkin, and D. Wheye. 1988. The birder's handbook: a field guide to the natural history of North American birds. Simon & Schuster/Fireside, NY. Life histories of species that occur in North America, plus essays on bird biology.

• González Diaz, J. and F. Collazo Torres. 2001. La avifauna endémica de Puerto Rico en video.

• Greenberg, R. and J. Reaser. 1995. Bring back the birds: what you can do to save threatened species. Stackpole, Mechanicsburg, PA. Extensive discussion of problems faced by migrant species in the Americas.

• Lack, D. 1976. Island biology illustrated by the land birds of Jamaica. Univ. of Calif. Press, Berkeley. Comparisons of Caribbean species, but lacks more recent DNA evidence.

• National Geographic Society. 2002. Field guide to the birds of North America, 4th ed. National Geographic Society, Washington, DC. General field guide for North American species, including many nesting birds and migrants to Puerto Rico.

• Nellis, D. 1999. Puerto Rico and Virgin Islands Wildlife Viewing Guide. Falcon Publishing, Helena, MT. Directions and access information to key wildlife areas.

• Ortiz Rosas, P. 1981. Guía del cazador: aves de caza y especies protegidas. Depto. de Recursos Naturales, San Juan, PR; Cooperativa de Artes Gráficas Romualdo Real, Guaynabo. Photos of game birds.

• Poole, A. and F. Gill, eds. The birds of North America. The Birds of North America, Inc., Philadelphia, PA. Monograph series with detailed life histories and extensive bibliography of species that occur in North America. http://bna.birds.cornell.edu/BNA/

• Raffaele, Herbert A. 1989. A guide to the birds of Puerto Rico and the Virgin Islands. Princeton Univ. Press, Princeton, NJ. Compact field guide with drawings of common as well as rare species.

• Raffaele, H.A. 1989. Una guía a las aves de Puerto Rico y las Islas Vírgenes. Publishing Resources, Inc., Santurce, PR. Spanish edition of above field guide.

• Raffaele, H.A., J.W. Wiley, O.H. Garrido, A.R. Keith, and J.I. Raffaele. 1998. Guide to the birds of the West Indies. Princeton Univ. Press, Princeton, NJ. Field guide covers the Caribbean region, with color drawings.

• Saliva, J.E. 1994. Vieques y su fauna: Vieques wildlife manual. U.S. Fish & Wildlife Service, Boquerón, PR. Photos of many species of birds as well as amphibians and reptiles.

• Schreiber, E. A. and D. S. Lee, eds. 2000. Status and conservation of West Indian seabirds. Soc. Carib. Ornith., Special Pub. No. 1.

• Tyrrell, E. Q. and R. A. Tyrrell. 1990. Hummingbirds of the Caribbean. Crown Publishers, NY. Excellent photos of all Caribbean hummingbirds, some of which are used in this book by permission of the authors.

• Wiley, J.W. 1996. Ornithology in Puerto Rico and the Virgin Islands. Pp. 149-179 in The scientific survey of Puerto Rico and the U.S. Virgin Islands: An eighty-year reassessment of the islands' natural history (J. C. Figueroa Colón ed.) Annals of the New York Academy of Sciences. Vol. 776. Succinct history and selected bibliography.

PHOTO CREDITS

T = top; M = middle; B = bottom; L = left; R = right ; u = upper; l = lower; * = captive bird.

Wayne Arendt—85M*, 86BR*.
Giff Beaton—Front cover, 2, 6B, 7, 10T, 10B, 22T, 24T, 24B, 30TL, 30TR, 32B, 35T, 38M, 39T, 39BL, 40BL, 41T, 41M, 42T, 43T, 44BR, 44BL, 45TR, 45ML, 45MR, 45B, 46B, 47BL, 47BR, 48TL, 48TR, 48BL, 49ML, 50BL, 50BR, 51Tl, 52T, 52B, 53T, 54B, 55Ml, 56M, 57, 58T, 59T, 60T, 60M, 61M, 62T, 62M, 64BL, 65T, 65BR, 66B, 67TL, 67TR, 67B, 68TR, 68B, 69T, 69B, 70T, 70BR, 71TL, 71TR, 71M, 72T, 72M, 72B, 73M, 74Tu, 74BL, 74BR, 75M, 75B, 79T, 87T, 88B, 89BR, 93M, 98MR, 99B, 100BR, 100BL, 101Tl, 105TL, 105TR, 105BL, 108T, 108M, 108B, 109T, 109M, 109BR, 110TL, 110TR, 110B, 111T, 112T, 112M, 112B, 114BL, 114BR, 114MR, 116T, 126B.
Pablo Blanco—56T.
Robert Cabello (Dallas Zoo)—121T*, 121B*.
Richard Crook—80B*.
Carlos Delannoy—54TL, 54TR.
Michael Donahue—49MR.
George Dremeaux—125T.
John Faaborg—Front cover*, 95B*.
Hank Golet—40BR
Bruce Hallett—Front cover*, 4B, 6T, 9T, 30B, 31T, 31M, 32M, 33B, 34T, 34B, 36T, 37B, 38BR, 43M, 44TL, 46T, 47TR, 48Mu, 48Ml, 49TL, 49TR, 50T, 51Bu, 51Bl, 53B, 59B, 63M, 64T, 69M, 70BL, 71B, 76T, 77T, 77M, 78T, 78M, 80T, 89TR, 89TL, 90M, 96B, 97TR, 103TR, 104T, 105BR, 106T, 106B, 107TL, 107TR, 107BR, 120T, Back cover top photo.
Earl Horn—119B.
Cameron and Angela Kepler—16B.
Greg Lasley—28, 51Tu, 74Tl, 86TL.
Hana Y. López Torres—61BL.
Ellery McClintock—101ML.
Javier Mercado—58T, 123T.
Leopoldo Miranda Castro—4T, 15L, 17B, 18B, 22B, 37T, 39BR, 61BR, 63T, 81M*, 90T, 97TL, 97B.

Luis Nieves—114TR.
Doug North—48BR.
Mark Oberle—Front cover, 9B, 14, 15R*, 20TL, 20TR, 20M, 21L, 21R, 23M, 25, 26T, 26M, 27T*, 27M, 40T, 42B, 44TR, 79B, 82T, 82M, 82B, 83T, 83M, 85T, 85B, 87BL, 87BR, 88TL, 88TR, 89BL*, 94B, 98TL, 99M, 101TL, 102T, 104B, 106M, 111B, 113T, 113B, 115Tl, 117T, 117B, 119ML, 119MR, 122BL*, 122BR, 123M, 123BL, 123BR, 124T*, 124B*, 125M, 125B*, 126T.
James Parnell—8, 74M.
Dennis Paulson—87M, 101MR.
Ken Riddle—58B.
Chris Rimmer—101BR*.
Carlos Ruiz Lebrón—47TL*, 101TR*, 102M, 116B.
Rafael Rodríguez Mojica (raromo@prtc.net)—11, 16T, 17TR, 21M, 23T, 24M, 25B, 27BL, 27BR, 52M, 55Mu, 60B, 66T, 86TR, 91TR, 92TR, 94M, 95MR, 100T, 100M, 107BL, 109BL, 113M, 114TL, 115M, 118T, 118BR, 122TL, 122TR, 126B, Back cover bottom.
T. Brandt Ryder—101BL.
Jorge Saliva—32T, 33T, 36B, 55B, 73T, 76M, 76B, 77B.
Father Alejandro J. Sánchez Muñoz—18TR, 18TL, 18ML, 19T, 19M, 35B, 38BL, 49B, 55T, 63B, 63M, 68TL, 81T*, 84B, 86BL, 92B, 93B, 94B, 95TL, 95TR, 96TR, 103TL.
Robert and Esther Tyrrell—17TL*, 18T*, 91TL*, 92TL*, 93T*.
U.S. Fish & Wildlife Service—Front cover*, 5*, 13*.
Luis Silvestre—115Tu.
Eduardo Ventosa—118BL.
Olivier Vimont—25T, 28T, 28M, 38T, 41B, 45TL, 53M, 56B, 61T, 64M, 64BR, 65BL, 68TL, 75T, 91M, 96MR, 96TL, 98TR, 99TR, 99TL, 115B, 119TL, 120M.
Jim Wilson—84T, 94T, 114ML.

SPECIES INDEX

ABBREVIATED INDEX
(Species index on page 129)

INSTRUCTIONS TO READ THIS CD-ROM

Follow the directions below if the CD-ROM does not open automatically:

PC
1) Find out which letter your computer assigns to your CD-ROM drive (e.g. D, E, F, etc.).
2) Insert the Puerto Rico CD-ROM into the CD-ROM drive.
3) Open your web browser (Netscape, Mozilla, Internet Explorer).
4) In the Location (Address) line, type: x:\home.htm (where "x" is the drive letter for your CD-reader).

MacIntosh
1) Click on the icon for this CD-ROM to open it.
2) Drag the file "home.htm" from the CD to your web browser.

INSTRUCCIONES PARA LEER ESTE CD-ROM

Siga las instrucciones a continuación si el CD-ROM no abre automáticamente:

PC
1) Averigüe cuál es la letra (D, E, F, etc.) que su computadora le asigna a la unidad de disco para el CD-ROM ("CD-ROM drive").
2) Inserte el CD-ROM sobre aves en esta unidad de disco.
3) Abra su navegador (Netscape, Mozilla, Internet Explorer).
4) En el espacio para la dirección, escriba: x:\home.htm (siendo "x" la unidad de disco o el "drive" que lee los CD.)

Macintosh
1) Pulse el icono para este CD-ROM para accesarlo.
2) Arrastre el archivo "home.htm" del CD al icono para su navegador.